THE MUSIC OF THE SUMERIANS

FRANCIS WILLIAM GALPIN

THE MUSIC OF THE SUMERIANS

AND THEIR IMMEDIATE SUCCESSORS

THE BABYLONIANS AND ASSYRIANS

Described and illustrated from original sources
with 12 plates, 6 pages music, cuneiform texts, and figures

BOOKS FOR LIBRARIES PRESS
FREEPORT, NEW YORK

First Published 1936
Reprinted 1970

STANDARD BOOK NUMBER:
8369-5234-0

LIBRARY OF CONGRESS CATALOG CARD NUMBER:
73-109625

PRINTED IN THE UNITED STATES OF AMERICA

PREFACE

THE world is growing older, older at both ends, for the past ten or fifteen years have seen a wonderful unfolding of its early history through the researches which have been so skilfully and successfully undertaken in Western Asia. Egypt no longer looms alone as the cradle of art and learning. Mesopotamia, with a culture in many respects surpassing it in fertility of imagination and ingenuity of invention, has staked a rival claim, and, as evidence, permitted us to view the greatness and splendour of her hitherto unknown past, the influence of which will probably be found to reach much farther westward than is at present recognized.

It is unnecessary for me to recall the diverse aspects of this Asiatic culture. The originality of its conceptions, the brilliancy of its embellishments, the delicacy of its handiwork and the astonishing modernity of its productions have been lavishly set before us in the published reports of excavators and experts and in the exhibitions which have been held of their discoveries.

Thus, through many avenues of past history, the paths of knowledge have been extended. A wider outlook stands revealed before the eyes of the potter, the metal worker, the architect, the builder, the artist and, I will add, the musician, for it is with this branch of art I desire to deal in the following pages. Something, it is true, has already been attempted to unfold the musical history of Babylonian and Assyrian days, and pioneers, such as Engel, Virolleaud and Sachs, deserve our thanks for breaking into unknown ground. For the wonderful age, however, which preceded these recognized periods and on which their foundations were laid, we have hitherto had but the literary researches made among archaic "cuneiform" tablets of clay by eminent scholars in works which are not usually familiar to musical students. Now, at last, hidden treasures of ancient cities and temples have revealed not only illustrations of the musical tastes of an older "Sumerian" people on seals and pottery, but actual specimens of the instruments they used and enjoyed, cleverly preserved to us by the most modern methods of salvage. In this connection mention must be made particularly of Sir Leonard Woolley's unrivalled explorations at Ur of the Chaldees and the richly illustrated and scientifically treated volumes of his Reports.

With these great advantages thus open to us, I have here endeavoured to give as detailed an account of the Music of the Sumerians and their immediate successors, Babylonians and Assyrians, as is at present possible. Dubious points still exist and I have not failed to note them; for another generation and other men's labours will, I hope, resolve them.

My subject I have taken down to the closing centuries of the pre-Christian era, when Sumerian was practically a dead language and the nation, as such, had ceased to exist for fourteen or fifteen hundred years. Well-ascertained dates are not wanting for the later periods, but for the earlier centuries considerable uncertainty still obtains. For these I have not hesitated to follow Dr Frankfort's chronology, as outlined in his treatise on *Archaeology and the Sumerian Problem* (1932), because it appears to be based on reasonable calculations. The date of the royal tombs and their treasures at Ur is therefore placed during the first half of the third millennium B.C. (*c.* 2700 B.C.), and this Early Dynastic Period, which may have begun with a Ist Dynasty of Ur (*c.* 3000 or 2900 B.C.), lasted till *c.* 2500 B.C., when it was succeeded by the Agade Period initiated by Sargon I. In the closing centuries of this same millennium we have the Gudea Period of Lagash (*c.* 2400 B.C.) with its interesting revelation of temple building and ritual, overlapping the commencement of the IVth and Vth Dynasties of Erech (*c.* 2380–2275 B.C.), which gave way to the IIIrd Dynasty of Ur (*c.* 2275–2170 B.C.) and the rule of Isin and Larsa (2170–1950 B.C.). The first Babylonian Empire occupies the earliest quarter of the second millennium (2040–1750 B.C.), until it was over-shadowed but not eclipsed by the Kassite invasion (1740–1160). The balance of power then passed northward and the famous Assyrian kingdom held the field till 625 B.C. Nineveh fell in the year 612, and the second Babylonian Empire lasted but a century (625–538 B.C.): then Median and Persian kings ruled the land, until in 331 B.C. they were dispossessed by the Greeks under Alexander the Great, with whom our story ends. We have, however, still to account for the centuries of civilization which elapsed before the Early Dynastic Period of the third millennium. There was the "Jemdet Nasr" Period, which immediately preceded it and from which we have our first indication of that peculiarly Sumerian instrument, the bow-shaped harp. Yet further in the distance are the "Uruk". (Erech) Period with its marked individuality in culture and progress, and the "Al'Ubaid" Period, stretching back into the simple life of the first settlers for an untold number of years. No dates with any probability can yet be given for these remote ages.

In the arrangement of the material provided I have followed the popular classification of my subject into (*a*) Instruments of percussion, placing the *autophones* and *membranophones* together under this heading, (*b*) Wind instruments or *aerophones*, and (*c*) Stringed instruments or *chordophones*. To avoid, moreover, constant footnotes and references to authorities in the text, I have grouped such notes under chapters and subjects at the end of the book: here too will be found measurements of specimens and other technical details.

The difficulty of allocating their proper names to the instruments discovered has been much increased by the fact that the original texts are written in cuneiform script: to consult them for due identification has therefore required a rudimentary knowledge, at any rate, of the Sumerian language. When we recall that to an unmusically-minded writer "harp" and "lyre" or "flute" and "pipe" are synonymous terms, it was quite unsafe to rely on translations: in every possible case I have consulted the Sumerian text itself. For the Assyrian language I have generally used the word Akkadian, both being of Semitic origin; they were practically alike, save in certain grammatical constructions: but in dealing with the days of the great Assyrian kingdom I have adopted the more usual word. It is with regret that I have been compelled to omit all quotations in cunei-form script, with its pictorial charm and old-world primness. Specimens, however, will be observed in the illustrations and on Plate I, our frontispiece, there are a few lines, inscribed between four thousand and five thousand years ago, in praise of Music and Song: they are taken from one of the clay cylinders of Gudea, the peace-loving king-priest of the third millennium B.C. at Lagash. In these words, which I have entitled "Music's Ministry" and given in transla-tion below, they breathe the eternal spirit of the Divine Art:

MUSICK'S MINISTERIE

> Kisal Eninnu ḫula siada
> Gig uru ibgar
> Šag ḫungada bar ḫungada
> Igi ir pada ir sigda

> To fill with joye the Temple court
> And chase the Citie's gloome awaie,
> The harte to still, the passions calme,
> Of weeping eyes the teares to staie.

Owing to the rapidity with which the Near East is unfolding the wider know-ledge of its past history, an exhaustive bibliography of published works on the subject would not only be out of place but largely out of date. For English readers, however, who wish to know more of the general history of these inter-esting peoples, with whom we are here dealing, the late Dr Leonard King's *Sumer and Akkad* (1910) and his *History of Babylon* (1915) will be found useful, while Mr Sidney Smith's *Early History of Assyria* (1928) will, at the same time, supply many valuable details more recently available. Mr C. J. Gadd's *History and Monuments of Ur* (1929) too is an attractive and able survey of the subject. A handy compendium is Sir Leonard Woolley's *The Sumerians* (1928); though also dealing in the main with the city of Ur, it outlines very briefly the general chronicles of the nation. In *Archaeology and the Sumerian Problem* Dr Henri Frankfort (Chicago University Press, 1932) faces the difficult question of racial origin and development, while Dr Gordon Childe's *New Light on the Most Ancient East* (1934) summarizes most of our present information. Such works as these, if read in connection with the notices which appear from time to time in the daily press and in the well-illustrated articles written by experts for the *Illustrated London News*, will help the ordinary student to keep abreast with the latest discoveries.

It would ill-become me to take to myself the credit of the research which the present work has entailed over several years. I am deeply indebted for the generous assistance I have received on all sides: especially for the interest, help and information which Mr Sidney Smith, Keeper of the Assyrian and Egyptian Antiquities in the British Museum, has shown and so readily given me, as well as for the encouragement which Mr C. J. Gadd, the Deputy Keeper, has afforded me, not only by his expert criticism, but through his excellent *Sumerian Grammar and Reading Book*, which has rendered my task possible. Although I would by no means wish to debit such authorities with all the conclusions here given, yet their approval has often heartened me, whilst their opinions, when adverse, have received, I trust, the consideration they deserve, and have been weighed against the musical, historical and ethnographical facts in my own possession.

For the interpretation of the notation set to the Sumerian Hymn I am solely responsible: spurred by the word "impossible", I have tried to express this ancient music in modern form on reasonable and acknowledged lines. Unfortunately we shall never meet with anyone who was present at its first performance and could vouch for its certitude: I must therefore leave it to my friends and critics to say whether they do not feel that these old strains, of nearly 4000 years ago and the oldest music we have, are indeed well-wedded to the yet more ancient words.

To Dr Langdon, Professor of Assyriology in Oxford University, to Dr Legrain, Keeper of the Babylonian Antiquities at the University Museum, Philadelphia, to Dr Moule, Cambridge Professor of Chinese, to Sir Leonard Woolley, to Dr Curt Sachs, to Dr Andrae of the Staatliches Museum, Berlin, to Dr Contenau of the Musée du Louvre, Paris, and to the Keeper of the Cairo Museum of Antiquities my sincere thanks are due for particulars I could not otherwise have obtained and for illustrations they have so generously allowed me to use. For many other details and illustrations here given I am grateful to the Trustees of the British Museum and of the Victoria and Albert Museum, the Conservateur of the Louvre, the authorities of the Babylonian and Musical-Instruments Museums, Berlin, to the Superintendent of the Museo Archeologico, Florence, to the Conservateur of the Museum of Antiquities, Istambul, to Messrs Putnam, to Baron von Oppenheim, Professor Herzfeld, Dr Frankfort and the Oriental Institute of Chicago University, and to Dr Ernest Mackay.

Nor must I forget the willing assistance which has been given me in my research-work by Mr F. G. Rendall, F.S.A. of the British Museum, the Rev.

A. Parrot of Paris, Mrs Volkmann of Berlin, and Miss Dorothy Cross of the University Museum, Philadelphia, with other friends, as well as the expert and artistic production of the results by the Cambridge University Press.

To my wife, who has carefully read both manuscript and proofs, I dedicate this little book in memory of a long and happy comradeship. Twenty-five years ago in *Old English Instruments of Music* I endeavoured to trace existing forms to early sources: I trust that my present effort may throw yet further light on the history of origins, for it is clear that the evidence provided by the forms of Musical Instruments plays an important part in this quest. It is not probable that a peculiar form of instrument was invented in widely differing or separated localities; it must presume a migration of a special material culture, and so a diffusion of another achievement in the long tale of human progress.

FRANCIS W. GALPIN

GM

TYPOGRAPHICAL NOTES

The Sumerian names of musical instruments are given in Roman capitals and, following the usual practice, the component signs of words and phrases are separated by hyphens for derivative and grammatical aid. In the quotation, however, transliterated in the foreword, the words are treated on ordinary linguistic lines. In the Creation Hymn the names of Gods and Goddesses are initialed for clarity with a capital letter and, as a key to vocal rendering, recognized contractions and elisions are frequently employed.

Akkadian and Assyrian names of instruments are placed in Italic type, as are also names of foreign extraction.

The small figures in the letterpress refer to the notes on the respective chapters at the end of the book.

The pronunciation of some of the less familiar transcription-signs is as follows:

ç = tsh	č = tsch	ḫ = kh	ḳ = q
ṣ = ts (z)	š = sh	ṭ = hard t	g is hard

The vowels sound as in Italian. A circumflex over a vowel denotes two similar vowels contracted.

CONTENTS

Chapter I

PERCUSSION INSTRUMENTS, *p.* 1

(AUTOPHONES AND MEMBRANOPHONES)

Chapter II

WIND INSTRUMENTS, *p.* 13

(AEROPHONES)

Chapter III

STRINGED INSTRUMENTS, *p.* 26

(CHORDOPHONES)

Chapter IV

SCALE AND NOTATION, *p.* 38

Chapter V

THE APPRECIATION OF MUSIC, *p.* 51

CONTENTS

Chapter VI

THE RACIAL ELEMENT IN MUSIC, *p.* 70

Musical instruments as national characteristics—theories of Sumerian origins—possible evidence from their musical instruments—additional note: the development and distribution of the bow-shaped harp.

CHAPTER I

Percussion Instruments

DRUMS, TIMBRELS AND RATTLES

IN treating of the arts of the Sumerians we must bear in mind that, although we are speaking of days nigh five thousand years ago, we are not face to face with a "primitive" race in the accepted meaning of that word. When the curtain rises during the fourth millennium B.C. we are introduced to a highly cultured and artistic people: centuries must have elapsed in their pre-history, wherever that was lived out, to have enabled them to attain to the standards of social amenity, skilled handicraft and ordered existence, which are the prominent features of their earliest appearance. In fact, we may truly say that the period, in which they now for the first time take their place in world history and progress, was for them their golden age—the culmination of unknown years of racial development. For, within a thousand years or so of their recognized appearance, decadence is beginning to set in, and, amid the strife of internal factions and external invasions, the curtain falls at last to rise again on other scenes and other ways.

Their cultural efficiency, however, was by no means lost to the world in which they had so ably played their part: their very speech became the religious tongue of many later centuries. In tracing therefore the history of their art there must be included in our survey many of the achievements of their immediate successors—Akkadians, Babylonians, Assyrians and Persians.

Dealing as we are in this opening chapter with what may be termed the simplest forms of sound-production—the instruments of percussion—we must not expect to find much trace of man's earliest attempts to soothe his savage breast by music's charm. Yet, as in all nations, even in our own, there are survivals still in evidence, so here too we may observe how rhythmic expression preceded the tonal art.

At Kish and at Ur, among some of the earliest remains of these dwellers in Mesopotamia, certain curiously curved blades of thin copper have been found, generally in pairs: at first they were considered to have been weapons of war but they are now recognized as "dancing sticks", the metal blade having been fixed to a wooden handle.

In one instance, at Ur, they were discovered in connection with the remains of a lyre, and on a gold cylinder-seal also found at Ur, as well as in mother-of-pearl inlay at Kish, their real use is shown. On the seal (Pl. II, 1), which dates from about the year 2700 B.C., a dancer to the strains of the lyre is depicted and, on either side, attendants clapping the curved sticks together in measured cadence.

On another seal (Pl. **V**, 5) we have the counterpart of the well-known *crotala*, as shown on predynastic vases in Egypt and illustrated by Loret in Lavignac's *Encyclopédie de la Musique* (Part I), while they also remind us of the boomerang-like clappers or the mere rib-bones of cattle—not to say of slain foes—which still figure in the rituals and war-dances of primitive African tribes. Perhaps we can hardly class them as musical instruments: but what is music without rhythm? Our regret is that their Sumerian name is not at present known.(1)

(*a*) DRUMS

In the drums, however, to which we now turn, there is a much higher form of art: the hollow log of wood or the empty gourd has been developed into an instrument not only rhythmic but tonal by the addition of a stretched skin. For, whereas to the ordinary ear the sound of the drum is accounted as mere noise, to the delicate appreciation of the Oriental the "note" of the instrument is not only a source of pleasure but distinctly tunable.

The common Sumerian name for the drum was UB—in Akkadian *uppu*, probably used generically: in order to distinguish it from other meanings of the same word, it generally bears the determinative prefix for "skin" or "leather", SU UB. The word itself originally implied either something "hollowed out" or "enclosed", and it corresponds to the Greek word *lephes* or *lepis*, a cup or limpet-shell. If we may judge by the cuneiform ideogram or sign used in the archaic period (Pl. **X**, 2), it was at that time a single-headed drum, while a later form of sign suggests that it then had straight sides (Pl. **X**, 17), the head being tapped by the fingers like the old Indian *Tabla* and many of the East African instruments. There seems to have also been a smaller representative with a bowl-shaped shell or body, the UB-TUR or "little drum", corresponding, according to the ideogram (Pl. **X**, 2), to the Syrian *Tabil* (Pl. **X**, 10) and the *Baz* used by the Dervishes (Pl. **X**, 14). At the Temple of Enki at Eridu there was an UB-ZABAR, i.e. of bronze. We read also of an ancient Chinese drum called *happu*, but it had two heads of skin and was carried on a pole or hung in a frame. The UB was used in solemn processions together with the double reed-pipe, timbrel and other drums.(2)

A still more interesting type of Sumerian instrument is the BALAG, which also had a smaller form, the BALAG-TUR.

Dr Yetts in his preface to the second volume of the *Eumorfopoulos Collection Catalogue* (1930) states, from his own experience in dealing with Chinese specimens, that "ancient script may often be found to yield clues towards the solution of archaeological problems, especially when things of everyday life are in question. The drum is a simple object fitly represented with a pictorial sign". Accordingly the archaic ideogram for BALAG (Pl. **X**, 1) shows us in the third millennium B.C. a sand-glass- or hour-glass-shaped instrument with two heads; even the suspending strap is hinted at: for this drum was played horizontally with both hands, not with sticks, as depicted in the seal impression from Ur (Pl. II, 5), where the broad collar of the carrying strap is prominent on the neck of the hindermost player. This was especially the Temple Ritual Drum and Ea or Enki, whose name is sometimes written with the BALAG sign, is the God of the Drum and patron of the chanting priest (*Kalu*). Its very shape links it with primitive worship, for in its barbaric form it was probably made of two human *crania*, like the Tibetan *Čang Teu* (Pl. X, 7) of the present day, taken from the skulls of slain enemies or of holy men. In substitution for such gruesome material half-gourds could be used, as in Malabar, and, in order to secure a surer fixing between the two hemispherical portions, a ring-shaped piece of bamboo stem was inserted: this still appears in the little Indian *Damaru* known as Šiva's Drum (Pl. X, 8) and in some of the African examples. The instrument is seen in its lengthened form in the Indian *Huruk*, in the Soudanese type (Pl. X, 9), and in the Chinese *Čang Ku* (Pl. X, 6), which is by them acknowledged to be an importation from "the western barbarians" of the second millennium B.C. and is held and played like the BALAG. As early as 2600 B.C. the Indus Valley Culture possessed it.

The Akkadian and Assyrian name was *balaggu, balangu, palagga* or *pelaggu* (cf. the Aramaic *palgah* and Syriac *pelagga*, a drum). The body was usually made of wood—cedar-wood is mentioned—and, as there are no traces of bracing cords as in later specimens, the skin heads were probably attached to the circular frame by wooden pegs.(3)

Several of the earlier Assyriologists considered that the BALAG was a lyre, because it was used to accompany the voice of the temple psalmist or chanter: but the ancient and still popular accompaniment to Asiatic song is the drum, and the word *napaçu* used in connection with the BALAG means "to hit or strike a blow". The art of drumming, however, which has received such minute attention in India, as Mr Fox Strangways has shown in his *Music of Hindostan*, is something far more than mere tapping; under the touch of a skilful player it can add intense meaning to the words sung. So we are told on the ancient tablets that the BALAG completed the song and joined in "the full music"; the singer to its accompaniment could "assuage the tears" and could "soften the sighing"; when used in joyous procession its sound "calmed and uplifted the men of the city". On the other hand it could be struck to attract the divine attention: for a Hittite ritual tablet (*c.* 1300) tells us that the *katraš*-woman (the cymbal player) took the drum (BALAG) and "thereupon summoned the gods".(4)

It was this mystic voice of the drum which led the Sumerians to link its sounds with the utterance of the Deity.

In the description of the restored Temple of Ningirsu at Lagash, which the IŠAG or priest-king, Gudea, beautified about the year 2400 B.C., we find great reverence paid to the BALAG. In the dream which he had previous to the commencement of the great work, he was told to make the sacred emblem, the divine sword and chariot, and also "the drum beloved by Ningirsu; its name UŠUMGAL KALAMMA (Great Ruler of the Land); the instrument which speaks with auspicious voice, which gives counsel unto the hero, who loves to make gifts". The time of its making provided a name-date for the year. The drum was entrusted to the care and use of a special officer, who also bore the honorific title of the instrument.(5) In Miss Densmore's description of the *Drum Religion of the American Indians* we find a somewhat parallel arrangement. Certain specified men may sing the Songs of the Drum, but only one may "speak" to it, and he is the chief, who keeps the instrument. In describing the ritual the chief said "sometimes my wife and I will have a little feast of our own beside the Drum and ask it to strengthen us in our faith and resolution to live justly and to wrong no one". In the same way Gudea's Drum was said "to confirm his counsels". This divine attribute is reflected also in the cult of the Sumerian kettledrum, the LILIS, which will be described later: to it was given a special place among the hierarchy of the gods. Even to this day the "Drum speech" is recognized by many primitive peoples; in Mandingo Land the natives imitate their own language by pressing the skin head or side-cords of the drum and so varying pitch and tone: or, by certain rhythmic beats, any desired message can be conveyed Morse-like. Among the Swedish Laplanders the Wizard's Drum was till the last century a fetish, and was used for divination in their old religious worship. In this connection it will be noticed that in the seal impression of the Agade Period (*c.* 2500 B.C.), illustrated on Plate II, 3, there is an altar of hour-glass shape standing in front of the Goddess (Ishtar). This altar is exactly like the BALAG Drum and is believed to have borne the same name: on it are placed offerings, which suggest an earlier time when the actual drum was so used. It may be that its shape acquired some special significance in relation to the worship of the Mother Goddess, for on an omen tablet of late date we read that the appearance in the *viscera* of the shape of "the timbûttu (BALAG-DI, a similar kind of drum) before my Goddess Ishtar" was to be considered a propitious sign "for the heart of my army will, with the help of the gods, be a rampart". A further account of this curious tablet is given on subsequent pages.

The BALAG must often have been of considerable size, for its sonorous note is compared to the bellowing of a bull and rightly described as "not conducive to sleep". In Europe it appears in Spanish MSS. of the eleventh and twelfth centuries of our era, probably through Oriental introduction.(6)

It assumed however another form, already mentioned, called the BALAG-DI (the Akkadian *timbûttu* or *timbpûtu*), no doubt smaller, which probably was "the singer's drum": but as its general shape was similar to that of the BALAG, it shared the same ideogram. An illustration on an Elamite seal (*c.* 1200 B.C.) shows it in the paws of a lion and accompanying the harp and double pipe in an animal orchestra.

This identification of the BALAG class of instruments with the drum is corroborated in an interesting way. The name *timbûttu* was given by the Akkadians to a species of cricket common in their country. Professor Landsberger, in *Die Fauna des alten Mesopotamiens* (1934), using the old idea that the drum was unworthy of the prominence given to the BALAG (which is, as we have shown, a mistake), translates the appellation *timbûttu egli* as "the Harp (?) of the Field". But the sound-producing principle of the cricket is not connected with any stringed instrument; it is of the drum type—in fact, it is a friction drum of original and beautiful design. The taut membranes (known as *tympana*), which underlie the leathery fore-wings are, through the lateral motion of the wings, set in vibration by a file-like nerve rubbing against the hardened surface which adjoins them. This principle, though it has been developed in various ways, remains the same whether a rosined hair is attached to the membrane or a roughened stick used. In these forms it has existed for long ages in India and in Africa, and has worked its way into Europe; the little friction drum found in Spain is actually called *Chicharra* (field cricket). Whilst we would not infer from this that the more developed forms were known in Babylonia, it certainly suggests that the friction-stroke, assiduously practised by the old Indian drummers and employed in our own day by tambourine players, was also used on the BALAG-DI. The ball of the thumb, swept across the drum-head with a slight pressure, raises the pitch of the note and produces the characteristic "cri" (*rigmu*) of the insect.

We find that the BALAG-DI or *timbûttu* was not only employed in the liturgies for which explicit directions are given, but was also used at feasts. It is also observed in the hands of women, for the grand-daughter of King Naram-Sin, Lipushiau, was appointed player of the BALAG-DI in the Moon God's Temple at Ur (*c.* 2380 B.C.). Probably the illustration, taken from a figurine found near Ur and now in the British Museum, represents this instrument (Pl. III, 7). The name BALAG-LUL, which is also connected with singing, seems to have been sometimes given to it.(7)

Another form of drum, which admits the use of the BALAG sign, is the DUB, and, bearing the determinative *erû*, it must have had "copper" in its construction; no doubt its shell was made of metal, an alternative use which we find also in the Indian *Damaru* (Pl. X, 8). The name seems to survive in the *Dudi* and *Budbudika* of India, with their metal bodies, and it may be compared with the Arab *Dabdab*, the Georgian *Dubdabi*, and the temple drum of Sanskrit days, the *Dundubhi*. Even the Hungarian drum-name *Dob* reflects the same idea, for it is evident that it is onomatopœic and derived from the sound of the instrument, which was probably small and with little resonance.

It is interesting to notice that, in the same way, the Old English pipe and tabor were popularly known as the whittle and dub. Moreover, the ancient Sumerian instrument was also used with the flute, for the word DUB or *eru*-DUB is associated with LUB or TI-GI-LUB which, as will be explained in the next chapter, denotes the vertical flute. Similarly, in the account of the musical instruments used in the Temple of Enki at Eridu, we find the BALAG and "the seven-note" flute coupled together; while a footnote at the end of a Babylonian liturgy informs us that it is "a litany for the BALAG and TI-GI"—drum and flute. At the present day the ritual dance of the Dervishes is accompanied by the vertical flute (*Nay*) and drum (*Baz*).(8)

We may here remark that, in harmony with the genius of the language, "BALAG" and "DUB" (without determinatives) are used to express also such abstract ideas as "lamentation" and "wailing", incident to the association of the drum with these observances: in the same way the name of the cross-strung harp, ZAG-SAL, is employed (without a determinative) to express the idea of "praise", in which it took its part.(9)

Very different from the BALAG and much larger was the A-LA, or, with its determinative, SU A-LA. The derivation of the name from LAL would imply that this big drum was "suspended" from a pole or post, or "hung" on an ornamental stand, like the Chinese drums. In the Carchemish relief (Pl. III, 1) it is seen supported by a man. It stood in the temple forecourt and was five or six feet in diameter: it was struck by two players either with the open hand or with a stick. In the poem, written about the year 2200 B.C. and already quoted, which deals with the temple music at Eridu, the fact is mentioned that at one time there was no SU A-LA, but one had now been "installed in its proper place".

In the Temple of Ningirsu at Lagash the combination of the A-LA with the TI-GI (flute) sounded, we are told, like "the raging of the storm"; and it may be that the so-called BALAG, to which on its being "set up in the forecourt" of the Temple of Baba on a New Year's Day was given the name of NIN-AN-DA-GAL-KI (Mistress of wide heaven and earth), was also a large drum, like that pictured on a fragment of Gudea's stele or column. This instrument is also well illustrated on two other relics of the third millennium B.C., viz. on the stele of Ur-Nammu (Pl. III, 6), now in the University Museum at Philadelphia, and on part of a steatite vase preserved in the Louvre at Paris: in the latter example the instrument is surmounted by a figure of Ea or Enki, the God of Music. The skin head, probably varnished, like that of the Chinese drums, to resist the weather, was attached to the frame when wet by wooden pegs: it dried taut; the peg-heads are visible on the circumference, as on the LILIS or kettledrum described later. Its sound is said to have filled with joy the forecourt of Eninnu, the Lagash Temple, and, when the ISAG, Gudea, performed the lustrations and divine petitions were offered, the A-LA with the horn (SÎM-DA) and the sacred drum (BALAG) "made the music perfect". No wonder that it could be said of the Enki Temple at Eridu that "to its lord by night it reverberates with thun-derous sound". We know that the NAR A-LA—the drummer—was considered an important person, for he is particularly mentioned. Another large drum appears to be alluded to on a Kassite cult tablet (*c.* 1500 B.C.) under the name SU GU-GALU (the great bull's hide).

At present we have no indication that these large instruments were employed in processions, although, in an Egyptian wall-painting at Bubastis of the XXIInd Dynasty, a very similar drum is shown on the shoulder of an attendant walking before the player, and a large drum appears in Hittite sculpture (Pl. III, 1) borne by a man. As with the BALAG, the making and setting up of an A-LA gave a name-date to the year in which it occurred: on a list of offerings made to a temple in the IIIrd Ur Dynasty (*c.* 2200 B.C.) ten measures of meal are credited to the A-LA and only two measures to "the great well".(10)

The last type of drum about which we have reliable information is the LILIS (*lilissu*). It evidently had two forms, large and small—the former stationary, the latter carried in processions (Pl. X, 11). From the illustration of the larger form, with the name placed over it, which a scribe has given to us on a late Babylonian tablet (Pl. III, 4), we should infer that one kind of LILIS was of the "goblet" shape, so generally found in Asiatic countries—or, to use Dr Yetts' terms, they were "footed" drums as distinct from "hanging" or "pillared" drums. If so, this type of portable instrument would have resembled the Arab *Darabukke* (Pl. X, 13) or the Telugu *Ghutru* (Pl. X, 12), both of which are made of wood or clay in goblet shape with a skin head at the larger end. A Theban painting of the XVIIIth Egyptian Dynasty gives us a picture of its place in joyous pro-cessions, and it was used at entertainments with the timbrel or tambourine called ME-ZE. A clay figure of the XVIIIth Dynasty, found at Dêr el Bahri by the Egyptian Exploration Society, apparently shows a seated Asiatic with a turban on his head beating with his hand a little "footed" drum which is held under the left arm. This probable example of the portable *lilissu* is in the British Museum. Of the larger form, made in bronze, we have minute details given to us in the Babylonian tablets found at Erech, and in the line-drawing on a tablet of priestly instructions, illustrated on Plate III, 4. It was a true kettledrum, its goblet-shaped shell resting on a short foot and low base, very similar in many respects to the modern Persian *Donbek* (Pl. X, 15). At the end of Chapter v are transcribed the more important details of its construction and consecration as given on the tablets, and it will be sufficient here to say that it was beaten with two sticks and, together with the bull from which its skin-head had been taken, was accorded divine honours. The skin-head was attached to the metal body by pins of hard wood driven through the skin when wet, into holes already prepared in the shell; the large heads of these pins were wrapped round with coloured wools and varnished; they are prominently shown in the illustration of the A-LA (Pl. III, 6).

Many African lake-district drums preserve the same method of affixing the head with wooden pegs and continue the like goblet shape (Pl. X, 16): in fact, this particular type of instrument appears among races of very early times, for Professor Kosinna in *Die Deutsche Vorgeschichte* has illustrated a Stone Age drum of similar shape which he dates about 2500 B.C.: here, however, the skin-head was affixed by cords passed through ear-shaped projections with eyelet holes: it must have been used in worship, for it is decorated with sacred signs. The Chinese "footed" drums, *Lei*, *Ling* and *Lu*, are used respectively to accompany the sacrifices to the spirits, to the gods of the soil, and to the shades of the ancestors: they are also beaten to ward off calamities, and the archaic script presents a sign-picture of them very like the standing LILIS (Pl. X, 5).

In the ritual used at Erech for the observance of an eclipse the copper LILIS had to be used with the double pipe and the single pipe: they raised a lamentation of grief and weeping for the darkened moon. The appearance too of the shape of this footed drum in the *viscera* at divinations is said, in a tablet of the Seleucid era, to denote peace and unity, for "according to one mouth the land will swell". A representation (Pl. III, 2) of this kettledrum occurs on a Babylonian plaque of *c.* 1100 B.C. in the British Museum(11).

(b) TIMBRELS

Leaving the drums we pass to their near relatives, the timbrels or tambourines, with shallow frames and usually with one head only. Amongst the Sumerians there were two types: The A-DA-PA (*adapu*) had a rectangular frame and perhaps skin-heads on both sides. A grain-measure of similar shape was called by the same name. The instrument was employed in the temples to accompany certain hymns and liturgies called after it. Dr Langdon in his paper on *Babylonian and Hebrew Musical Terms* gives the names of five psalms so to be sung, and mentions an entire liturgy, to the God Anu, described as an A-DÂP. On a tablet of the Ur-Isin Period (*c.* 2100 B.C.) is preserved a hymn to Enlil in honour of King Dungi with this subscription "a psalm of the High Priest, a song on the A-DÂP to Enlil".

It is evidently shown with the sistrum on the harp inlay of Ur (Pl. VIII, 2), where it is laid on the knees of a jackal-headed creature and tapped with the fingers as an accompaniment to the lyre. It is also just discernible on the lap of a sistrum-player in a seal impression of the Agade Period (Pl. II, 3). There are instances of its employment about the middle of the third millennium B.C. It is again exhibited in processional use on a bronze from Niḥawand in Persia (Pl. VI, 3), where it is preceded by the upright harp and followed by hand-clappers. It also appears on an Elamite relief at Malamir as well as on a Kassite seal of c. 1300 B.C. in the Louvre. On the seal too of Queen Shubad (c. 2700 B.C.) the same instrument is probably depicted at a banquet together with the small bow-shaped harp (Pl. II, 4). As the name is sometimes preceded by the determinative URUDU, there must have been some "copper" about it; may be "jingles" or a metal-covered frame. It seems to have given its name to the *Adufe* or *Duff*, a square-shaped timbrel, credited by Arabic tradition to Tubal the coppersmith as its inventor. Tuwais, the great Arabian singer of the seventh century A.D., accompanied himself on the *Duff* alone: at that time it was not only used in hymns of praise or sorrow but also figured in martial music. Dr Farmer informs us that in early times the name *Duff* was used for any kind of tambourine, whether with jingles or not: the present-day square Moroccan *Daff* or *Deff* with two heads is without them (Pl. X, 18). With the ADÂP may be compared the single-headed and octagonal Indian *Duffde* and the Hebrew *Toph*. Praetorius in his *Syntagma Musicum*, vol. II (1618–20) gives an illustration of a square two-headed "Muscovite" timbrel (Pl. X, 19).(12)

The other type of tambourine was called ME-ZE (*mezu* or *manzu*) or, with the "skin" determinative, SU ME-ZE. It was in the shape of a ring, with one head. Is there here a possible derivation of the English word "timbrel" (through the earlier form "tymbyr") from the Assyrian *timbu*, "a ring"? Perhaps it is rather too far a cry. The A-DÂP and the ME-ZE were closely connected, being equated together in descriptions; though the latter was not only associated with the temple liturgies and incantations but was certainly also used at feasts and in popular gatherings with the drums, lyre, double pipe, etc. The instrument is well shown on an early Babylonian figurine in the British Museum (Pl. III, 5), where it is in the hands of a priestess. Sometimes it was held and played on the left shoulder (Pl. III, 3), and at Tell Halaf it is depicted in a limestone relief as being played by a bear and by a cat. It was often held aloft (as at Tell Halaf), and, on a Babylonian *Kudurru* or boundary stone of the Kassite Period (c. 1400 B.C.) and now in the Louvre, it is flourished by a maiden, who heads a procession of seven men playing on the long-necked lute or *tanbur* and attended by various kinds of animals. It appears too on a figurine from Mohenjo-daro (c. 2600 B.C.).

In the same way the Arab *Dâire*, the Persian *Dayere*, and the Caucasian *Dahare* are employed at the present day: they are however furnished with "jingles".

The psalms sung to the ME-ZE were probably called "ME-ZI-MA", and an interesting light on its ritual use is afforded by the ceremonial glosses on some of the temple hymns which were intended to indicate to the chanting priests or their attendants the proper form of accompaniment. Thus we read "the *Mezu* is to be removed", i.e. *tacet*; "the *Mezu* is to be used"; and, as a final *fortissimo*, "for the second time (the repeat) the *Mezu* should be ready". It seems to have been especially linked with joyful outbursts, for in the desolation, which ultimately overwhelmed the land, the psalmist laments that in E-sagila at Babylon "the *manzu* sounds not, the *balagga* sounds not". The great liturgy used in the Temple of Enlil ends with two psalms sung to the *manzu*: it was also associated with the double-pipe in holy chants, and on a Phoenician ivory of about the year 800 B.C., found in Assyria, it is shown triumphantly borne before two psaltery players and a performer on the double-pipe (Pl. VIII, 5).

Sir Leonard Woolley (*Ur Excavations*, vol. II, 1934) records that in the grave of the Prince Meskalamdug (*c.* 2700 B.C.) he noticed close to the coffin a quantity of small "conical bosses" of thin copper sheeting, laid over wooden cores; with them there were plentiful traces of wood and also of some substance which looked like leather or skin; he suggests that they formed the remains of a drum. This appears to be very probable and from the position of the cone-like articles we should say that it was a single-headed instrument probably of the timbrel (ME-ZE) type (Pl. III, 3), about 20 inches across the head, and originally placed in the grave aslant. It would correspond to the large Arab *Ghirbāl* (Pl. X, 20), the modern *Bandar*, which had no jingles and is described by early writers as "like a sieve": being considered an official instrument, it was used at proclamations: had not the Prophet himself said "Publish the marriage and beat the *Ghirbāl*", although he had a strong dislike for anything with jingles.(13)

(c) RATTLES

The most interesting instrument in this autophonic section is undoubtedly the *sistrum*. It had been thought that Egypt was pre-eminently the home of this historic rattle, but the harp-inlay found at Ur of the earlier part of the third millennium B.C. and the seal impression of the Agade Period at the middle of the same millennium show its very ancient use in the land of Sumer and Akkad. As will be seen, however, from the illustrations (Pls. II, 3; VIII, 2), the shape of it differs from the typical Egyptian instrument. Dr Curt Sachs describes it as the "spur" shape, distinct from the "temple" and later "stirrup" shapes, which abound in the Valley of the Nile and, according to his view, appeared there about 2500 B.C. (Pl. X, 24, 25). From its method of construction the Sumerian sistrum is evidently a more primitive type; indeed, on the seal impression from Ur (Pl. II, 5) the third performer in the dance orchestra seems to be shaking a larger and still earlier form of this same rattle. If it came from Egypt, its importation must have been in pre-historic times.

In the Egyptian Museum at Berlin a unique example of a wooden "spur" sistrum is preserved (Pl. X, 21): it was found at Assiût and the date is said to be about 2160 B.C.: at that time the Princes of Siût appear to have been in close touch with Babylon. It will be noticed that the "jingles" are formed of metal bars instead of rings: and remains have been discovered at Ur of portions of a highly decorated instrument: the end of the handle and the points of the fork are tipped with ornamental knobs, and the six "jingles" of 8-shape, with two holes for the cross-wires, are made of cut shell. In the Tiflis Museum there is a sistrum of this "spur" type from the Caspian district, with which Mesopotamia was in close commercial touch at an early period (Pl. X, 22); and in Abyssinia the same shape is still in use for ritual dances (Pl. X, 23).

Unfortunately the Sumerian and Akkadian names for the sistrum cannot at present be traced. It is somewhat strange that an instrument so closely connected with religious worship should apparently receive no mention in the priestly tablets. We can only conjecture that either its employment was discontinued at an early date or else was restricted to the particular use of certain temples, like the horn (sîm-da).(14)

A simpler form of rattle was the KATRAL. It has been pointed out that, in the Hittite Legal Code, there is written "if anyone steals the bridle, reins or copper Katral of a horse or mule he shall" (receive punishment). Here KATRAL evidently means the little disks or jingling pieces of metal commonly suspended in the East from the necks of horses, mules or camels. The word can therefore be correlated with the Indian Khattâli (metal castanets, square or round), or with the more developed Kartâl and Karatâla (cymbals). It may be that the rattle-like instrument held downwards by a pig in the Tell Halaf reliefs is an early form of the KATRAL. The use of true cymbals, however, in Mesopotamia is of comparatively late date, though not so late as it was in Egypt, where, according to Dr Sachs, they did not appear until the Hellenistic Period. Illustrations of flat-shaped cymbals and others of conoidal shape, corresponding respectively to the Jâlra and Tâla or Karatâla of India, are found on Assyrian reliefs of the seventh century B.C. (Pls. VI, 7; X, 26). Such instruments or their simpler predecessors were in use for the temple worship: we have already mentioned the incident of the Katraš-woman striking the sacred drum to summon the gods: on a Babylonian plaque (c. 1100 B.C.) in the British Museum such a woman is represented with her cymbals accompanying a performer on the kettledrum (Pl. III, 2).(15)

Small bells for suspension from the horse or mule trappings seem to have been frequently used in Assyria, for specimens in bronze with or without iron clappers have been discovered, varying in size from $1\frac{3}{4}$ inches to $3\frac{1}{4}$ inches in height. Some clapper-less examples have the hole in the crown immediately under the little suspension loop so characteristic of early Chinese bells (Pl. III, 8). A more important bell, though but little larger (3¾ inches in height and 2¼ inches in diameter) and evidently of Babylonian or Assyrian origin, although its original location is unknown, is preserved in the Asiatic department of the Staatliches Museum at Berlin. It is made of bronze and the sides are decorated in relief with the symbols of Ea (the great magician of the gods and friend of mankind), Nergal and Ninurta; it was probably suspended from the neck of the high priest by a ring through the two loops and used in incantations for averting evils and calamities (Pl. III, 9).

On the old tablets we read of a temple instrument called NIG-KAL-GA which, as it is preceded by the "copper" determinative URUDU, must have been made of that metal. A Kassite tablet (c. 1500) implies that it was a cult utensil on which a noise could be made: the suggestion has therefore been put forward that it was a large bell used for similar purposes as the specimen at Berlin: it too was connected with Nergal, the blazing sun, sword-bearer of Enlil, Lord of the Nether World and God of the Plague and all sicknesses.

There is a legend that one of the solar destroying-powers, probably identical with Nergal, agreed to withhold his attacks if he received due recognition, declaring that "the singer who sings of my deeds will not die of pestilence: in the temple where my tablet is set up and the people proclaim my name, he will dwell in safety". The idea that the sound of a bell is powerful in warding off evil spirits long survived, as a Christian custom, in "the Passing Bell" at death and in the mediaeval practice of ringing the church bells during a thunderstorm. In the Tibetan temples and monasteries a bell called *Drilbu*, engraved and ornamented with figures of the deity, is used during times of prayer for the like purpose.

With the NIG-KAL-GA is associated the large drum SU GU-GALU, mentioned in the same Kassite cult-tablet, and it may have been hung, like the Chinese bell, *Yung Chung*, in the forecourt of the temple and opposite to the large drum, A-LA, which would then correspond to the Chinese drum, *Chin-Ku*.(16)

CHAPTER II

Wind Instruments

FLUTES, PIPES AND HORNS

THE unravelling of the Sumerian wind instruments has been rendered somewhat more difficult through a loose application of technical terms by translators of the old records. This is especially true of the first two sections in this chapter, for the word "flute" has been applied indiscriminately to whistle-sounded instruments and to those played by means of a vibrating reed. We have therefore consulted the original cuneiform texts and, in the following pages, will use the term "flute" for the first type and the word "pipe" for the reed instruments.

(a) FLUTES

The flute *par excellence* of these early ages is the vertically-held simple reed-tube, sounded by blowing across one of the open ends. In Mesopotamia it was generally called TI-GI (Akkadian *tigu, tegu*) or sometimes KA-GI (mouth-reed) and was highly esteemed in the temple ritual. Gudea, in the later half of the third millennium B.C., gives special instructions to the Director of Music in his newly-restored Temple at Lagash, "to cultivate diligently flute-playing and to fill the fore-court of Eninnu with joy". In the same period there is a somewhat similar instruction to the Musician of the Temple at Eridu, where it was used in incantations.

On a seal impression found at Ur (*c.* 2700 B.C.) appears an illustration of the flute-player who is performing music for the ritual dance together with the lyre, sistrum and drum (Pl. II, 5). In a subsequent chapter on the scale we shall deal more fully with the construction and capabilities of this instrument: it will suffice to say here that it had three finger-holes, equidistant from one another (Pl. XI, 1), and, by the help of the first and second registers of the harmonic series, could produce a diatonic scale of seven notes with a sharp or tritone fourth: this scale could be extended into a second octave.

The flute TI-GI is therefore called also the "IMIN-E" ("the seven-note"). In a poem in praise of the Temple of Enki at Eridu (*c.* 2200 B.C.) we read "the musician on the 7-note brings forth a plaintive sound", and again, "into the hallowed forecourt let the musician duly bring the drum and 7-note". In the account of a festival at the Temple of Ninab (*c.* 2000 B.C.) we are told that the sound of the great drum, the "7-note" and the sacred drum was heard in the city (probably Nippur). Other descriptive names were also employed, such as "the long-reed or instrument" (GI-GID, GI-BU, GIŠ-SÍR) or "the large reed" (GI-DIM) as contrasted with the much shorter reed-pipe. In a liturgical hymn to Dungi there is, at the close, a "tacet" cue for the player—"GI-GID (long flute) let be". On a late tablet in her honour Ishtar says "the *Kalu*-priests, all of them, stand around with the flute" or, as the more correct translation would seem to be, "with flute and drum (LUB-DUB-TA)", an expression explained in the first chapter under the term DUB. On a similar tablet the goddess is compared to "the long-flute (GI-BU) and the reed-pipe whose sound is pleasant". Such appreciation it is natural to expect, for the TI-GI is "the sweet *mon-aulos*"—the love-flute of the Greeks, and identical with the *Ugab* of the Hebrews, notwithstanding its translation as "organ" in the Authorised Version of Genesis iv. 21. There is also a curious reference to the character of this instrument in the Jewish *Bereshith Rabba* (50), where we read "the angels said unto Lot, there are flute (*ugab*)-players in the land and the land ought to be destroyed": Gesenius (*Heb. Lex.*), connecting the word with *agab*, "to blow", adds that this is also applied to inordinate affection.(1)

The vertical flute is certainly one of the oldest, if not the oldest, of all wind instruments. It appears to have preceded the well-known "Pipes of Pan"; for, although the little row of river-reeds is so familiar to us now from the many illustrations given in Greek and Roman art, and from its widespread use in Eastern Asia and the islands of the Pacific, not to mention its association with the merry pranks of Punch, the Panpipes do not occur, so far as we can at present discover, in the earlier culture of Mesopotamia. Dr Sachs relegates their appearance in Egypt to the Greek Period of the fourth century B.C.

Illustrations of their old-world predecessor will be found on an early Sumerian seal in the Louvre (Pl. IV, 1), on a palette from Hierakonpolis in the Ashmolean Museum, Oxford, and on Egyptian wall-paintings of the Vth Dynasty (c. 2500 B.C.), where it is frequently shown in the much extended form common in later times, though at present we have no instance of the use of this longer type in Mesopotamia. Flute-playing was called in Egypt *Seba*; *Sebi* means in Coptic "a flute" (Pl. XI, 2). Correlated types are recognizable in the ancient Chinese TIK, TEK or TI (Pl. XI, 1), of which more will be said in a subsequent chapter; also in the Annamite *Tieu*, the Arab *Nay*, the old Madagascan *Sodina* (three holes with complete diatonic scale) and the Roumanian *Kaval*. In India, Africa and also amongst the American Indians the same simple music-maker is still in request. In Japan the Chinese flute retains the old name, *Teki*.(2)

Did the Sumerians and their immediate successors know the principle of the whistle-head, which so facilitates the production of sound from the vertical flute and gave us, in mediaeval days, the recorder and the flageolet? We have reason to believe they did, for at Birs Nimrud near Babylon a whistle pierced with finger-holes was discovered about the year 1860 and was presented to the Museum of the Royal Asiatic Society, London. Fortunately Engel, in his *Musical*

Instruments of the Most Ancient Nations (1864), gave an illustration and a detailed description of this valuable relic; for it is now lost (Pl. **IV**, 2). It was found in association with several little figurines and was made of baked clay: though of the flute class, it is, in reality, of the *ocarina* or resonator type, as the lower end is closed. When the two holes were covered by the fingers the note C (we are told) was produced and, by raising the fingers, the notes E and G: by blowing harder A might be reached. Engel also observed that by closing the *left* finger-hole a note about a quarter-tone lower than the E, obtained by closing the *right* finger-hole, was produced. It is impossible, without seeing the actual specimen, to say whether this difference in pitch was intentional or due to some obstruction which prevented free speech: but, from facsimiles we have made to scale, it is interesting to find that by half-opening the finger-holes a semitone lower than the full pitch is in each case obtained: using the right finger-hole, there is the progression C, E flat, E, F sharp, G, A: but if the left finger-hole (flat) is used C, D, E, F sharp, G, A are easily sounded, suggesting that the hole was purposely flattened to facilitate the production of D natural. The whole instrument was only three inches in length: in Engel's illustration it is mistakenly figured upside down, giving a somewhat grotesque appearance.

We are far from insisting that the Sumerians knew the mechanism of the whistle-head in the earliest period, although neolithic man used it and, in yet more remote ages, Siberian mammoth-hunters introduced the principle at any rate into the reindeer grounds of Eastern Europe. At Babylon it was probably at first "cross-blown" like the vertical flute: if so, it was similar to instruments found in the Harappa Culture (Indus Valley, *c.* 2600) and the primitive *Hsüan* or Chinese *ocarina* of the present day (Pl. **XI**, 3); but the mechanical mouthpiece is wanting in the Indus Valley civilization.[3]

As to its actual name we have just this possible reference on a tablet of the Greek Period (*c.* 300 B.C.), now preserved in the Ashmolean Museum, Oxford, containing a bi-lingual Ishtar epic. According to Mr Sidney Smith, the God of Heaven, Anu, is addressing Ishtar in her capacity as a goddess of battle and says: "Let the arrow pass through, piercing heart and entrails like an *uku*". The cuneiform ideograms employed for *uku* mean "to pipe on a flute", and Mr Smith adds "may we translate—like a blast (on a pipe)?" But the ideograms seem to imply also a sound "striking" or "overpowering" and "high in pitch". Only a short instrument, of the whistle type, could give these effects. It is worth while noticing that a Bantu word *uku* is used for "blowing a wind instrument" and that the sound of the whistle blown by these African tribes in war and incantations is believed by them "to penetrate the heart (of the evil-doer), who is frightened and will sink and die". Here we appear to have the counterpart of Anu's appeal against the foe.

So the name of this Babylonian whistle may be *uku* and, in its form, be compared with the Kirghis *Čor* (also found in East Turkestan) and the African *naka*; the whistle anciently used by the Mongol cavalry may have been similar in its intention. The possibility of the whistle-mouthpiece being in existence in early times in China is maintained by Tsai Yü in his work *Lü Lü Ching I* (1596). In our own day the same principle is preserved in the *ocarina*, which was originally a child's toy sold at fairs. Like its Assyrian prototype it had a whistle-mouthpiece, two finger-holes and was made of baked clay. It is said that its name "little goose" is due to its sometimes bird-like shape. In France it is called *coucou*.(4)

(b) REED PIPES

The earlier instruments included under this section may have been of the single-beating reed or clarinet type, in this respect corresponding to the old Egyptian *Mait* and the modern *Arghoul* and *Zummarah*, but the question is discussed in the notes to Chapter IV. So far as we know the single pipe was the first to appear, as we should naturally expect, and it is well exhibited on a lapis-lazuli seal found in one of the most ancient dynastic tombs at Ur (*c.* 2700 B.C.), where a monkey, surrounded by animals in Elamite style, is playing it beneath a tree (Pl. II, 2). The difference between this instrument and the TI-GI or longer vertical flute is distinctly shown by the angle at which the instrument is held: this is necessary for the insertion of the vibrating tongue of the reed within the mouth. There are other seal impressions showing a similar subject and from the records we gather that the pipe was sometimes made of copper. The name among the Sumerians appears to have been NÂ (in Akkadian *nabu*), a word still preserved in the Arabic *Nāy* which includes both flute and reed instruments, as we find from such names as *Diyanai*, *Suryanai*, or the Indian *Sânai* and the Persian *Nāy-i-ambân* (a bagpipe). It also corresponds to the Greek *Aulos* and the Akkadian *Ḥalilu*, whence the Hebrew *Ḥalil*, a reed-pipe.

In the Hymn to Ishtar, quoted under the previous section, its pleasant sound is linked with that of the flute. But its plaintive character appears to have predominated and we find the names GI-ER-RA or GI-IR-RA (*nabu*, "to lament"; *nababu*, *qan bikiti*, "the wailing reed") given to it. In a liturgy to Enlil (*c.* 2000 B.C.) we are told that "the shepherd sits down to play the reed of weeping (GI-ER)", reminding us of Chaucer's "pypés made of greené corn, as have thise litel herdegromes that kepen bestés in the bromes". It is recognizable too under the name GIŠ GÙ-SÌR or "the instrument with the crying voice". In a Sumerian penitential hymn the suppliant says "like the reed NÂ, I am in sadness", and in a lamentation by Ishtar for Tammuz she wails "a reed of lamentation (GI-ER-RA) is my heart". The *Ḥalil* pipe of the Hebrews appears to have been employed in the same way for, in showing the utter desolation and destruction of Moab, the prophet Jeremiah (xlviii. 36–38) cries "mine heart shall sound for Moab like pipes...there shall be lamentation upon all the housetops and in the streets thereof".(5)

The combination, however, of two single-pipes must soon have suggested itself, for in a private grave at Ur, a little later than that just mentioned, but still of the Early Dynastic Period, portions of a double-pipe, twisted and bent, made in silver, together with fragments of another similar pipe, have been discovered: there are four holes on each tube and, though they date from as early as c. 2800 B.C., they may be compared with the Egyptian pipes in the Museum of Leyden University (Nos. 476 and 479), and the Lady Maket pipes of the XVIIIth Dynasty now preserved at Berlin. They are very slender, being about $10\frac{1}{2}$ inches in length and only $\frac{3}{16}$ inch in diameter (Pl. IV, 3). No reeds were found with them; but the scale is given in Chapter IV. A terra-cotta figurine (Pl. IV, 4) from Nippur of the Ist Babylonian Dynasty (c. 2000 B.C.) shows that they were held in the V-shaped and divergent way depicted in the Egyptian wall-paintings and like the Greek double-*aulos*. These pipes are now in the University Museum, Philadelphia. The Sumerian name for the double-pipe was ŠEM, in Akkadian *halhallatu* (the "double" *halilu*): the instrument is frequently mentioned in the temple ritual. It was often made of copper or bronze, as well as of silver: when of wood or reed it seems to have been called GIŠ HAR-HAR, for the archaic ideogram suggests the form of two tubes ("pierced" or "bored") placed side by side, though not necessarily bound together throughout their whole length as in the Egyptian type of *Zummârah*.(6)

We find that a special class of ceremonial hymns was known as ER-ŠEM-MA or pipe songs, for, like the single-pipe, the ŠEM was played in penitential processions: "to the House of the God with crying lament, and prayer let us go: the priest sings the song of woe with the hallowed little-drum (*uppu*), the hallowed kettledrum (*lilissu*), with the double-pipe (*halhallatu*), the timbrel (*manzu*) and the hallowed drum (BALAG)"—so they kept the fast in the eighth century B.C. In a tablet for the ritual observance of an eclipse—probably written in the Seleucid Era (c. 300 B.C.) for the temple at Erech—the copper *halhallat*, the copper ER-ŠEM-MA, and the copper *lilissu* are mentioned together—"the double-pipe, the single-pipe, and the kettledrum to the eclipsed moon a lamentation of grief and weeping let them raise". Undoubtedly the instrument was not confined to such scenes of sadness, for it appears at the joyous foundation of a temple and takes its part in festive processions as it did in Hebrew minstrelsy. We may note that in the Sardinian *Launedda* illustrated in the Spanish Cantigas of the thirteenth century A.D., we have a triple-pipe of the same class.(7)

A third interesting type is the *KITMU*, on which the reed was probably "covered" (Akkadian *katâmu*) by a cap of rush, gourd, wood or horn, an improvement on the earlier practice of placing it inside the player's mouth. It is mentioned in a list of late Semitic songs on a tablet found at Asshur and forms the accompaniment to seventeen love-songs to be sung by women. It appears to have also been called *KANZABU* (cf. Hebrew *kanaz* or *kanas*, "to cover over") and takes its place with the double-pipe and stringed instruments in a hymn of praise to the Goddess Nanâ, written in the days of the later Sargon (eighth century B.C.). We can find no early mention of it. The "covered" reed is displayed in the Indian *Tubri* or *Poongi* (Pl. **XI**, 5), which is said to be a very ancient type of instrument, with double tubes and a gourd cap. In the Ionian Islands pipes, both single and double, are found "covered" (Pl. **XI**, 6): the Russian *Brielka* has a wooden cap, the Keltic *Pibgorn* or hornpipe (Pl. **XI**, 7) was horn-capped, and it is also reported from China (Pl. **XI**, 8), Java, and the Basque Provinces, where it is called the *Alboquea*.

The Greek *Physallis* and perhaps the *Symphonia* (mentioned in Daniel, ch. iii) may also have been so constructed, as precursors of the bagpipe: the question of the *Symphonia*, however, is fully discussed in an additional note on "Nebuchadrezzar's Orchestra" (ch. v). The mediaeval *Platerspiel* (Pl. **XI**, 10) too remains an echo of bygone efforts.

With this "covered" type some writers would connect the Etruscan, Greek and late Egyptian *Subulo* or bulb-pipes (Pl. **XI**, 9). The rush bulb, of which a few remains have been found, was placed over the beating reed and not only allowed more free vibration than when held inside the mouth, but also helped to catch the moisture impeding its action. On the other hand, M. Loret considers these fragments as parts of the double-beating reed itself, the growing rush-stem, from which it was cut, having been contracted by binding artificially, in order (we would suggest) to give more "spring" to the split and flattened end; a cincture of some sort is generally found on this type of reed. Until, however, a perfect example of this curious bulb-mouthpiece is discovered, its actual purpose must remain uncertain.

If the first explanation be adopted, it would certainly be less difficult to explain the well-known feat attributed to Midas, whose "mouthpiece", on one of the pipes, broke during a Pythian contest, though he continued his performance and gained the prize. The Scholiast, in his notes to the Twelfth Ode of Pindar, says "he played on his pipes alone like a *syrinx*" (a vertical flute)—a difficult task indeed, unless his pipes were of large bore, and one which must have affected the intonation. If it were the bulb-tip which gave way, the reed within might have been sounded by blowing on the broken end, or the two reeds placed within the mouth according to the old style.[8]

Another pipe, fitted probably with a single-beating reed, was called *PÍTU*. The Sumerian ideogram, DUN, implies something "bored" or "hollowed out", but with it we find associated a word *kippatu*, which means "curved". The *PÍTU* therefore was probably cf the Phrygian type with a semicircular up-turned end or bell. Originally no doubt this was an attached horn, as in the present-day Ionian Islands pipe—whence the Greek name *Keraulos* or hornpipe: afterwards it appears to have been constructed of wood in a similar way as the Krumhorns of mediaeval times. Mr Sidney Smith mentions the interesting fact that in an early Sumerian list of supplies brought to a temple, including sheep and goats, were *DÙN-GI GU*, which may well be translated "hollow-reed bent-pipes". In the list they are fancifully attributed to the mythical hero Gilgamesh, the man of many labours, of whom we shall have occasion to speak more fully in the next section of this chapter. These "bent" pipes were employed singly or in pairs and were especially associated with the Asiatic worship of the Mother-Goddess Cybele. An excellent illustration is given on Plate XI, 11, from the monument of a priest of Cybele now in the Capitoline Museum, Rome, and dated *c.* 125 A.D.: behind it is placed the *Gingras* with its double-reed, which was also attached to the same worship. On a Susian figurine (Pl. IV, 5) attributed to the eighth century B.C. there is displayed a "bent" pipe: it has been considered part of a bagpipe and, if so, it would be the earliest illustration of that delightful instrument at present known: for the so-called Hittite bagpipe of Eyuk (*c.* 1000 B.C.) is very doubtful and suggests simply a performing bear-cub with a gipsy attendant playing the long-necked guitar—a common enough scene.

Dr Langdon thinks that the Assyrians may have had a true bagpipe in the seventh century B.C. and that it is mentioned under the name GI-DI (Akkadian *takaltu*). The word *takaltu* is supposed to mean a "case" or "bag", in which wood or leather played some part. It was used by the priests. As Dr Langdon himself is doubtful on this point, we must leave the question of the bagpipe, so far as Assyria is concerned, till more definite information is obtainable, for the so-called Chaldean bagpipe (*Symphonia*) mentioned in Daniel, ch. iii, comes to us in a text the date of which is very uncertain. The other word GI-DI reminds us, however, of the names of the Turkish and Arabian bagpipe *Ghaidâ* or *Gajda* (Pl. XI, 13), and the Slovak *Gajdy*, though by derivation *Ghaidâ* is said to mean "soft" or "gentle".

With the single-reed of the *PÍTU* we may compare that of the South American *pito* which is of the same *Zummârah* type. In the Ishtar epic, already quoted, the *kippe* ("bent" instruments) are mentioned and the translation may be given as "Ishtar, make the encounter and the struggle 'bend' like the Phrygian pipes".(9)

The last reed instrument of which we must speak is the *IMBUBU*, certainly a double-beating reed pipe, tapering in shape and played either singly or in pairs. It was also called *malilu*, which corresponds to the Latin *tibia* (a leg bone) and may have been used loosely in a generic sense. The pipe no doubt was introduced from Syria where its name was *Abuba* (Arab *imbub*) and its female performers were known in Rome as the *Ambubajae*. It is identical with the *Gingras* (Pl. **XI**, 11) which was high-pitched: the pipe, being conical, would sound an octave above the cylindrical *ḥalilu* and *ḥalḥallatu*. In the hymn of praise to Nanâ (*c.* 720 B.C.) it is mentioned under the name *malilu* in combination with the covered pipe and stringed instruments.

According to Dr Sachs this double-reed pipe was introduced into Egypt *c.* 1500 B.C. and its identity with the *Gingras* is strengthened by the fact that, whereas Adonis, the hero of the Cybele worship, was called at Perga *Abôbas*, he was known to the Phoenicians as *Gingras*. It has also been ascertained that this form of worship had a close affinity with that of Ishtar and Tammuz, a late name for the goddess being *Gingira*. This may be the intended reference in the Ishtar epic "Goddess of the hurly-burly, follow battle as though it were the music of the *passu*"; for Mr Smith says the *passu* was a reed-pipe of the oboe type, and this double-reed instrument was frequently used in martial display and as an incentive to bravery. It is often depicted on the Assyrian bas-reliefs (Pl. **VI**, 8); it appears on the carved ivory box from Nimrûd (Pl. **VIII**, 5), and the Hittites and Cypriotes knew it well, its somewhat conical outline distinguishing it. Correlated forms of the present day are the Arabian *Zamr* and *Suryānai* or "Syrian pipe" (Pl. **XI**, 12), the Persian *Zurna* and the Chinese *Sona* (introduced). In the Indian *Sânai* we have the double instrument, which in the Middle Ages appeared too in Europe as one form of the Chalemie or Schalmei. The latter, in later times, became the *Shalm* or Shawm of merry England. The British Museum exhibits a Tibetan specimen of the *Zurna* richly decorated with coloured stones; but this is nothing new, for in a Sumerian hymn Ishtar says "on the Day of Tammuz play for me on the pipe (*malilu*) of lapis-lazuli and pearl".

It is interesting to find that on the ninth- or eighth-century tablet from Asshur, already mentioned, which contains a library-list of liturgical hymns and popular songs, the headings, which give the name of the instrument to be used as the special accompaniment, place the name in the plural for the *PÎTU*, *KITMU* and *IMBUBU*. Undoubtedly these three kinds of pipe were often played in pairs, like the double-pipes called *ḥalḥallatu*, a use which is borne out by illustrations on bas-relief, sculpture and in painting, as well as by the survival in Eastern countries of a similar practice at the present day.(10)

(c) HORNS AND TRUMPETS

For our quest in this important section we have found Mr Sidney Smith's monograph, from which quotations have already been made, an invaluable starting-point on the linguistic and philological side. For the early history of horns and trumpets is wrapt in mystery, and Dr Sachs contents himself with the statement that the trumpet first appears in Egypt under Thothmes IV (*c.* 1415 B.C.) and that the name *šneb* given to it is "New Egyptian". Budge in his *Egyptian Dictionary* gives, it is true, another name for it, viz. *thupar*, which has been compared with that of the *shophar*, the ram's horn instrument of the Hebrews: but the word *thupar* is now pronounced non-existent. Yet from the beautiful specimens of these instruments still extant, dating from the fourteenth or fifteenth centuries B.C., as displayed by the finely engraved silver trumpet with gold mountings discovered in the grave of Tut-ankh-amen (*c.* 1350), shown on Plate **XI**, 25, and by the *Lurs* and horns of the Bronze Age which have been unearthed in Central Europe, Scandinavia and Ireland, it is quite evident that a long period of time must have elapsed before such artistic skill was brought to bear on the far more primitive instruments. That we have but few early illustrations of such instruments is perhaps not surprising, for, as we shall see, the horn type of sound-producer has either been enveloped in sacred mystery or else used as a potent means of exorcising demons and scaring foes. In a Mari temple (*c.* 2700 B.C.) two Sumerian figures were found, holding curved objects made as blowing-horns.(11)

It is therefore most fortunate that on an archaic Sumerian tablet we are given an evident account of the making of an instrument of this kind. The tablet, which has been translated and annotated by Mr C. J. Gadd, was found at Ur and, although dated at the end of the Larsa Period (*c.* 1950 B.C.), it refers to tradition of remote antiquity: for it describes one of the many "labours" under-taken by the Sumerian hero, Gilgamesh, in his search for the plant which would secure his immortality. The story in brief is this: Gilgamesh, finding a hollow tree in the root of which a serpent had made its nest, proceeds to cut it down with his axe: the birds, which have built in the hollow branches, take flight and he kills the serpent. He then plucks up the tree by the root and, after offering the top of it to his patroness, the Goddess Inanna, he makes out of the root a *PUKKU* (Sumerian GIŠ RIM) and out of one of the branches a *MEKKU* (Sumerian GIŠ E-AG). The men of the city, who have flocked out to witness the proceedings, are commanded to keep silence; only the *PUKKU* and the *MEKKU* are to utter a sound. His lament is made and a night-watch set: then, in the words of the tablet,

> On the spot, where the *PUKKU* lay, he drew a circle;
> The *PUKKU* he set up before him, and went into the house.
> In the morning he viewed the place where the circle was drawn;
> The older people did not open their lips;
> But, at the crying of a little girl
> His *PUKKU* and *MEKKU* fell down into "The Great Dwelling".
> He put forth his hand, but he could not reach them;
> He put forth his foot, but he could not reach them;
> Gilgamesh shed tears; he turned pale of face;

"O my PUKKU! O my MEKKU!
Who will call my PUKKU from the earth?
Who will call my MEKKU from the underworld?"
His servant Enkidu says to him
"My Master, why are tears wept? Why is thy heart sore?
To-day thy PUKKU has called *me* from the earth,
Thy MEKKU has called *me* from the underworld."

Now from this description we may certainly gather that the PUKKU and MEKKU were hollow pieces of wood and that, together, they formed a magical instrument which would make a sound; for the power of "calling" is attributed to them, even to bringing back the faithful Enkidu from the realms of the departed.

The instrument, though described in two parts, was evidently one. This is shown by the fact that, whereas in the first and last portions of the poem above quoted the MEKKU and the PUKKU are both mentioned, at the critical point of the story only the PUKKU is spoken of. From other literary texts it is clear that the two words imply similar objects, connected in some way but not exactly identical, although, in the syllabaries, both words are given as the equivalent rendering of the same Sumerian ideogram GIŠ ELLAG. When they are mentioned together, different signs are necessarily employed, and one of the signs used for MEKKU suggests something associated with the mouth (GIŠ KA-RÂII); hence we conclude that the MEKKU—the hollow branch—was used for the tube of the trumpet (the MEKKU was sometimes made out of a reed), and that the PUKKU or BUKKU, made from the trunk, was the "bell" of the instrument, which stood on the ground when the instrument was "set up". Even to-day in Persia the name *Boug* or *Buki* is given to a small horn (Pl. **XI**, 15) and the Arabian *Būq* or *Buque*, though now a war-trumpet, was not considered such a martial instrument in the eighth century of our era, but one for common use. The archaic root BUK—"to puff, bellow or roar"—underlies many of the Asiatic trumpet-names. Here then we find probably the earliest notice of the horn type of instrument: in Africa it is still frequently made of the hollowed branches of trees, often (as shown in Plate **XI**, 22) with a larger wooden end attached as a "bell". Wooden horns too survive in East Finland (Pl. **XI**, 14), in the Swiss alphorn, the Rumanian *Bucium*, and the Russian *Rog*; they are still used in many districts of Central Asia. The word *kizallu*, employed in this connection, suggests the "leg-bone" horns of Tibet (Pl. **XI**, 16), or that sometimes the reed or wooden tube terminated in a "gourd", round or curved like that on the Abyssinian *Malakat*, which has crept down the east coast of Africa as the *icilongo* (Pl. **XI**, 24). On a Sassanian dish, found amongst the treasure of the Oxus (sixth century A.D.), there is a representation of a man blowing on such an instrument; the upward curve of the gourd attached to the tube, which is bound round, gives a pointed resemblance to the Etruscan and Roman *Lituus*, which was from earliest days connected with sacred and magical rites. Burmah and Uganda provide examples also of horns or trumpets consisting of a reed tube with either a gourd or buffalo horn termination (Pl. XI, 18). It will be observed that the tablet-story makes no mention of the making of a vibrating reed in order to produce the sound. The *PUKKU*, *MEKKU* and *KIZALLU* are named in the Ishtar Epic as martial instruments.(12)

Another early form of this type of instrument must have been the natural horn of an animal and we find the suggestion of it on the cylinders of Gudea (*c.* 2400 B.C.): it is there called the sîm or si-im (in full si-im-da, and on a later tablet, si-im-du), the ideograms meaning "horn with breath" or a "blowing horn". There is also another rendering of the word sîm—the compound ideogram being si-mu, that is, a "horn to call", of which the Akkadian translation is *šahâlu*, "to call, to roar": and, for the reduplicated form, *nabû*, "to summon" or "proclaim". In the chapter on the Appreciation of Music we shall deal more fully with the use and purpose of this call-horn. Another Akkadian name is *ṣaddu*, which, as Bauer has shown, implies something similar to certain appearances of the Moon and Jupiter, probably their phases, in which they look like crescents and so horn-shaped. By the middle of the third millennium, however, the sîm was made in metal, for the "copper" determinative is placed before the name; and it is also included in an inventory of copper articles. From the days of Ur-lama (*c.* 2275 B.C.) and of Bur-sin (*c.* 2200 B.C.) temple receipts for a copper sîm-du and a special receipt for a copper sîm-da for Ningirsu, patron deity of Lagash, are extant: later still we read of a sîm made of gold. The instrument, at any rate at Lagash, was used with the large drum a-la in the temple forecourt and considered "full music"—on a Hittite bas-relief from Carchemish, now unfortunately broken up, a large drum and a horn are so depicted (*c.* 1250 B.C.) and are illustrated on Plate III, 1. It corresponds both in shape and use to the ancient Indian *Schringa* (called in Bengal *siṃha*) which, though made of copper, still retains the primitive horn shape (Pl. XI, 17). Another name, akin to the word *kizallu* already mentioned, has been suggested by Mr Sidney Smith for this particular shape, viz. gi-sal, which, on a tablet descriptive of the Temple of Enki at Eridu (*c.* 2200 B.C.) is said to "make a noise like a bull"; the word seems to imply that it or part of it was made out of a gourd and had "a V-shaped opening".(13)

A later and perhaps more interesting instrument, however, is the karan (Akkadian *karanu*), of which we have particulars in a letter addressed by Dušratta, King of Mitanni, to the Pharaoh, Amenophis III, on the occasion of the betrothal of his daughter, Tatuḥepa, to the Egyptian monarch (*c.* 1380 B.C.). Amongst the multitude of gifts he sent, and of which he took good care to specify the value, were two karan, the *pattu* (reed or tube), corresponding to the older *MEKKU*, being bound—probably with willow bark or bast—and the *kizallu* (gourd or bell), the older *PUKKU*, made of wood overlaid with gold: one of the instruments was also mounted with two gold bands. These were evidently trumpets for war-like purposes, for the name survives in the Persian *Karana* (Pl. **XI**, 23), still frequently made of wood, and the Indian *Karna* (Pl. **XI**, 26), both straight trumpets: the name is also found in Sanskrit records. The mention of their being "bound" (*abzu* from *abašu*, "to bind") is peculiarly striking, as this practice is seen in the "rings" of the Mari horns, and on our alphorns and herdsmen's horns (Pl. **XI**, 14): it is necessary, in order to prevent the splitting of the reed or the opening-out of the two halves of the wooden tube. The shorter form of the KARAN was used in Egypt (Pl. **XI**, 20), and it appears on a Hittite bas-relief (Pl. **XI**, 21). Miniature models in gold have also been found in the mounds of Tepe Hissar (Damghan) and Astarabad in Persia, dating from the second millennium B.C. (Pl. **XI**, 19): it may be they were placed in the graves as military or civic emblems: or perhaps for some mystic purpose, such as summoning the spirits of the departed: the little earthenware horns found with burials in the Egyptian Fayûm may reflect the same idea. A somewhat longer instrument (about 27 inches in length) and more closely resembling the Egyptian *šneb* (of the Tut-ankh-amen type), the Greek *Salpinx* and the Roman *Tuba*, is portrayed on bas-reliefs (Brit. Mus.) of the time of Sennacherib (701–685 B.C.). It was em-ployed for signalling to slave labourers who, in this particular scene, are en-deavouring to drag a colossal bull into position (Pl. **IV**, 7). The name of this long trumpet is thought to be *LABBANÂTU*, and Mr Sidney Smith has discovered a mention of its use in siege operations by Sennacherib in Palestine, where it sounded the assault. It is given as a translation of an ideogram equated also with the *MEKKU* previously explained. On concluding this account of the trumpets we may perhaps add that the supposed illustrations of such instruments in Egyptian wall-paintings as early as the Vth Dynasty (*c.* 2700 B.C.), given by Lepsius, are erroneous.(14)

Engel, in his *Music of the Most Ancient Nations*, states that we might expect to meet with the CONCH or shell-horn in Assyria. It is an instrument of undoubtedly high antiquity and connected especially with religious rites. We have fortunately been able to locate a specimen amongst the collection of antiquities from the ruins of Nineveh preserved in the British Museum. It is shown on Plate **IV**, 6, where the mouth of the shell, which has been broken off, has been sketched in. The point of the shell, however, retains the characteristic "cutting off" which marks its use, and the edges are worn smooth by the lips of the old-world player. Notwithstanding its age and frail condition, the instrument can still give its sound. It is the shell of the Asiatic *Tritonium variegatum*.

This form of horn—for the channel is really conical and not cylindrical as in a trumpet—is found in very distant parts of the world, not only in India (where it is the Sanskrit *Ananta-vijaya*), but in Persia, Afghanistan, Tibet, Annam, Burmah, Borneo and the Pacific Islands. Even Croatia, on the one hand, and the Incas of Peru, on the other, appropriated it. In India, where the Hindi name is *Schankh*, it is considered the instrument of Vishnu and is practically confined to the temple rituals, punctuating the recitations of the priests and calling to prayer: in Persia, however, it is now used as a summons to the bath. A monograph on the distribution of this instrument is being prepared, and one of the earliest illustrations of it is to be found on the eastern gateway of the Sanchi Tope (first century A.D.).(15)

CHAPTER III

Stringed Instruments

HARPS, LYRES AND LUTE

WHEN estimating the standard of culture to which a nation has attained we naturally turn to those details which demand constructional aptitude and display artistic appreciation. In the realm of musical instruments these would certainly be found in those stringed instruments which we are now to consider. For, while there is no disparagement intended of the earlier efforts of mankind to create enjoyment by rhythmic sounds or to animate the dance with the melody of flute and pipe, yet, whether as an accompaniment to the voice or in the beauty of their workmanship, the harp, lyre and lute stand pre-eminent.

On these the Sumerian artists certainly expended their best efforts and the highly ornamented instruments which have been found at Ur reveal, not merely the care and esteem with which they were regarded, but a manifest desire to increase their capabilities and to improve their mechanism.

The violin type is of course absent, for four thousand years were to elapse from the dawn of Mesopotamian history before India made its great gift to the world and the lute-like *rebabs* gave forth music under the touch of the bow, or gaunt *kemangehs* yielded their drone-like accompaniment for Arabian singers: on the other hand, the Sumerian public were spared the tortures which "rascal fiddlers", with untuned ill-played instruments, were in later days to inflict on suffering humanity.(1)

(a) HARPS

We set these instruments in the foremost position because we consider that from a Sumerian point of view they were the oldest and most characteristic.

The general name given to the harp on the tablets is GIŠ ZAG-SAL or the wooden "cross-strung" instrument (Pl. V, 3, 4 and 5) for, being bow-shaped in outline, the strings passed across from the upright arm to the horizontal soundbox, giving it the shape, known to the Sumerians, of an "open triangle". Genouillac, in a note on certain hymns in honour of the kings of Isin, points out that as the word *pitnu* has been established by Zimmern as meaning "a cord or string", the phrase *pitnu ša* ZAG-SAL, which occurs on a tablet, must refer to the gut strings of the instrument.

This form of harp, which takes pride of place in any list of instruments described in the ancient records, was also called the AL (i.e. "sound" or "music") and a psalm in its honour is extant, entitled "A meditation concerning the AL", which describes its mythical history and character. Its institution is ascribed to the great god, Enlil, who also gave directions for carrying it. Its head was made of lapis lazuli and its voice, with the deep tones of its strings, sounded like that of a horned bull. Its sound-chest (lit. "fulness") was in width like a well-conditioned farmer; to it hymns of fate were recited; it glittered as the stars; it was holy; by day in the temple it uttered speech, by night it poured forth song: the heroic God Ninurasha made it for Enlil, and the Goddess Nisaba tendered her advice, while Enki, God of Music, sang its praises. To this ancient poem the scribe of the tablet adds two notes; he tells us that the AL was the instrument for Enlil's fateful decisions and also that GIš AL "expresses" or "denotes" GIš ZAG-SAL. As we have already said, the word ZAG-SAL is also used in an abstract sense, meaning "glory" or "honour", and is found at the end of those laudatory hymns which form a distinct class of their own: but when so used, the determinative GIš, placed here, is omitted.

This description, fanciful though it may appear, can be applied in detail to the large harp (Pl. V, 3) found in the royal graves at Ur and dating from the earlier part of the third millennium B.C. The end of the sound-chest is decorated with the head of a calf; the tapering chest itself is deep and wide, very unlike the shallow resonance-chamber of the lyre (Pl. VII, 1): the only difference is that the finial at the head of the upright arm is made of gold, and the instrument was therefore classed at times with gold objects, whereas the head of the harp described by the poet was of lapis lazuli.

This large temple harp had from eleven to fifteen strings, specimens of both kinds having been found at Ur, and in one hymn we find mention of "a great great harp" The strings were of gut like the traces of those found on the lyres: they were not tuned by revolving pegs, but, passing over metal guides (a distinctly Sumerian improvement), were twisted round the arm and tightened or loosened by hand, as in the present-day African representatives of this bow-shaped instrument (Pl. XII, 7, 8), and in its Burmese survival, the *Soun* or *Saun* (Pl. XII, 3). The strings were either plucked by the fingers or struck with a large plectrum and it was sometimes played with the flute (KA-GI).(2)

Besides this fine example of Sumerian art, simpler and smaller specimens are also shown in the seal impressions of the Early Dynastic Period (Pl. II, 4), on yet earlier votive slabs found at Khafage, representing festal celebrations (Pl. V, 4), and on an archaic Ur seal (Pl. V, 5). But whereas the large harp was either rested on the ground or placed on a stand by the player, as so frequently seen in the Egyptian wall-paintings, the smaller instrument could be carried and played in processions. On a very early diorite vase (Pl. V, 1, 2), of which the remains were found at Bismya, the ancient Adab near Nippur, we see two musicians, the foremost with a seven-stringed bow-shaped harp marching before a royal personage and followed by a second player with a five-stringed instrument, while on the seal from Ur (Pl. II, 4) a similar harp with only four strings is shown. Too much credence, however, must not be given to the details of such small representations as these, for the artist often had to adapt his picture to the space provided. The name allotted to this little harp was, we believe, the *MIRÎTU*: it will be noticed that whilst the large instrument was played with the upright arm resting on the shoulder, as shown by the calf's head decoration on the front of the Ur specimen (Pl. V, 3) and the Egyptian type (Pl. XII, 5), the *MIRÎTU* was held with the bow-shaped neck outwardly, as in the African representatives of the present day (Pl. XII, 7, 8): it was certainly the more primitive form. Mention is made of it in a poem in praise of the Temple of Enki at Eridu (*c.* 2200 B.C.) with other instruments, the large ZAG-SAL coming first and the GIŠ *MIRÎTU* last together with the GIŠ *SABÎTU* or seven-stringed lyre. The name is of particular interest for it is the combination of a Sumerian expression GIŠ MI-RU or MU-RU with a common Semitic ending: GIŠ RU is correlated with the word *tilpanu*, meaning "a bow", for which the usual name is GIŠ PAN or BAN. Dr Langdon considers that the instrument is also mentioned with the lyre (AL-GAR) on the Gudea cylinder of *c.* 2400 B.C. At any rate we here appear to have the archaic name for this bow-shaped harp, which from the earliest times was known in Egypt as the *ban, ben* or *bain* (Pl. XII, 4, 6) (the "t" often written at the end is only the feminine affix), and survives in the Indian *Bîn* and *Vina* and probably in the Cambodian *Kin* (Pl. XII, 15). On the Buddhist *topes* at Sanchi and Amaravati (100 B.C.–120 A.D.) this harp is figured (Pl. XII, 1). The Siamese name for it, *p'in*, as well as the Indian *pinaka* (a musical bow), seems to imply that it was the original bearer of a name which, according to Dr Coomaraswamy, was afterwards transferred to another instrument derived from the bow, namely, the long-necked Indian *Vina* with a finger-board. We have dealt more fully in a note appended to Chapter VI with the history and distribution of this primitive harp, which has travelled through distant fields far away from its original Asiatic home. In Egypt in the first half of the second millennium B.C. we find it played *on* the shoulder, a position apparently peculiar to that time and country.

Though we have failed to trace the name BAN or PAN, as applied to this instrument, in any Sumerian records, there remain in their language, however, two words which seem to tell the tale of those older days, viz. GIŠ PAN-TAG-GA, "to hit or strike the PAN" and LU GIŠ PAN-TAG-GA, "a PAN striker". The sign TAG, that is "to strike", would then bear the meaning of the German *schlagen*, a technical term for playing on a stringed instrument with a *plectrum*, which was used, as we see from the Bismya vase (Pl. V, 1, 2), in the earliest example we have of the bow-shaped harp. The Buddhist *topes* too show the same manner of playing, which is also expressed by the Sanskrit word *tad*.

The *MIRÍTU* is evidently related to the Hebrew *nebel*, which was so called from its gourd or bottle-like sound-chest, and also to the Greek *nabla*, the Roman *nablium*, and the still surviving Nubian *nanga*. A charming illustration of this little harp in the later period is given in one of the well-known wall-paintings at Pompeii (Pl. **XII**, 2).(3)

Beside the bow-shaped harp, however, which has failed to hold its own amongst more civilized nations, we find another form of the instrument which became very popular in the Assyrian days and at that period must have been "the king of instruments". It was not a new invention, for it is well shown in the hands of a muse or goddess on a terra-cotta figurine (*c.* 1900) found at Sippar (Pl. **VI**, 6). It has been suggested that an archaic pictograph ḪUL (Pl. **X**, 3), meaning "to rejoice" or "joy and gladness", was derived from its use at great festivals. If so, it must have come into its popularity at a much earlier period. It certainly appears at Niḥawand (Persia) at the close of the third millennium (Pl. **VI**, 3) and it may have been at home in Elam or in Iran from remote times. The pictograph however may be merely a conventionalized representation of the ancient ZAG-SAL. We find its Assyrian name, at any rate, on a late Babylonian tablet written to commemorate the restoration of the city and its temples in the seventh century B.C., where we read "may its height be hymned with the *zaḳḳal* (or *ṣaqqal*) and may men sing of its loftiness". It bears the determinative for "wood" and as the archaic reading of the signs used for the name of the instrument is SI-SA, which means "to be straight or upright", it must refer to this up-standing type of harp on which the strings are set more *vertically* and not crosswise as on the ZAG-SAL. The *ZAḲḲAL* is depicted in its full development in the well-known representation of the Elamite orchestra, which welcomed at Susa their new king appointed by the conqueror Ashurbanipal in 658 B.C. (Pl. **VI**, 8) and which is now in the British Museum: it was also probably the instrument used at Nineveh to celebrate Esarhaddon's victory, though on this point the text is somewhat doubtful.

The name *ZAḲḲAL*, pronounced in Babylonia "zaggal", was nasalized, according to a common rule with double letters in Chaldee and Arabic, as *Čangal*, whence comes the Pushto *Changal*, shortened in Persian into *Chang* or *Chank*, the name for this same upright harp in that country. In Pushto, as in Persian, the word is also used to denote "the fingers extended as a claw"—an idea evidently taken from the position of the harpist's hands. From the name too arise the Indian *Čank* and the Arab *Jank* as terms for the same instrument.

Engel, in his *Music of the Most Ancient Nations*, mistook the little dots of decorative inlay on the sound-chest of this harp for tuning pegs (Pl. **XII**, 10). It was tuned, of course, by tightening or relaxing the strings as they passed round the lower horizontal rod, in the same way as on the ZAG-SAL. The number of strings varied greatly, though on this point we must again remember the artist's limitations as regards space, and the difficulty of representing minute details in the material used. On an example from Sippar there are four strings only; at Nihawand seven strings: at Malamir on the famous rock carvings (seventh or eighth centuries B.C.) fourteen strings: in the Elamite orchestra and on the Assyrian reliefs of the same period fourteen to twenty-one strings are shown: holes for twenty-one strings also appear on the late Egyptian specimens of a *ZAKKAL* preserved in the Paris Louvre and also in the Musik instrumenten-Museum at Berlin (Pl. VI, 1, 2). On these large harps, with a length of about three feet for the lowest string (as shown by comparative measurements and the Louvre and Berlin examples), the pitch of this string would be about C or D below our bass stave, and, with a scale of seven diatonic notes (which will be explained in a subsequent chapter), the compass of this twenty-one-string harp would provide three series of seven sounds each, like the well-known Chinese system. The upright harp in this western Asiatic type is shown on Egyptian wall-paintings and statuettes; it seems to have been introduced with other Asiatic fancies in the XVIIIth Dynasty and, owing to its peculiar shape, is called by Dr Sachs the angle-harp (*Winkelharfe*). It is also found on Cypriote pottery and on Greek vases: it travelled before the seventh century of our era to China (Pl. XII, 11), probably through Buddhist influence; but the Chinese themselves considered it a barbaric instrument "not to be cultivated"; in the thirteenth century we find it in Moorish Spain (Pl. XII, 12) and it appears to have lasted in Turkey till the sixteenth century. It will be noticed that the sound-chest rises *above* the arm or string-rod; and it is interesting to observe that the bow-shaped harp in Egypt assumed a very different form of development: for in the Egyptian upright harp (Pl. XII, 5) the sound-chest is *below* the projecting arm or rod, like the Scandinavian and Keltic harps and the modern instrument.

In nearly all the Asiatic and kindred types the front pillar is wanting, though signs are not lacking to show that, in course of time, the need of some means of increasing the rigidity of the framework was recognized (Pl. XII, 13, 14, 15).(4)

It is a usual practice amongst Orientals to name their instruments by the number of their strings: we have, for instance, the Turkestan *Dutar*, the Indian *Sitar*, the Afghan *Pančtar*, the Persian *Čartar* and *Častar* with two, three, five, four and six strings respectively. We observe the same idea in the Hebrew *Shalish*, mentioned in 1 Samuel xviii. 6, which was not a triangle, but an instrument with "three" strings (Assyrian *Šalaštu*)—in fact, a *tanbur* with the long neck like a lute, described later. In Mesopotamia a similar method obtained and there was an instrument of the harp kind called *ESIRTU* or the "ten"-strings. Dr Langdon gives a list of twenty-three love songs for accompaniment on the *eširtu* and, besides the ordinary *nebel* or harp already mentioned, the Hebrews had also a *nebel ásor* or "ten"-stringed harp.

Bearing in mind that the Sumerian bow-shaped harp was played with a long plectrum, we may surely infer that its derivative, the Assyrian triangular harp, shown so frequently in the bas-reliefs with nine or ten strings, was the *nebel ásor* or *eširtu* (Pl. XII, 9). Representations discovered at Eshnunna, of the opening years of the second millennium B.C., show the transforming process, and an early example from Nippur of the Ist Babylonian Dynasty (*c.* 1900) is seen on Plate VI, 4. A comparison with the primitive bow-shaped harps on the Bismya vase (Pl. V, 1, 2) will prove how closely this later instrument is allied to the earlier, both in method of playing and manner of holding; they were both forms of the *nebel*. An Egyptian specimen of this Asiatic ten-stringed harp is preserved in the Museo Archeologico at Florence (Pl. VI, 5).

Into the usage made of all these harps by the Sumerians and their successors it is needless to enter here as more details will be given in a subsequent chapter: they certainly enjoyed a prominent part in temple services and royal processions as well as in the domestic life of the people, and were united with the lyre in hymns of praise, paeans of victory, rhapsodies of heroic deeds and love songs for the merry-makings.(5)

(b) LYRES

In addition to the large and small harps the Sumerians made use of the lyre in several shapes and sizes. The name of the most important form appears to have been GIŠ AL-GAR or "the wooden instrument which makes music". The lyre differs entirely from the harp in having the strings stretched over or attached to a bridge placed on the sound-board, instead of passing into the sound-chest itself. A careful distinction must be drawn between the AL-GAR and the AL or ZAG-SAL, described under the previous section; as they are mentioned together in a poem in praise of the Temple of Enki at Eridu, there can be no question of co-identity.

Of this fine instrument we have many illustrations both in inlaid work, sculpture and on seals, as well as several highly ornamented specimens, covered with gold or silver, found by Sir Leonard Woolley at Ur (Pl. VII); but at the same time we have representations of far simpler and smaller instruments, sometimes held horizontally instead of upright, and placed in the hands of more humble musicians, both men and animals (Pls. VI, 7; VIII, 2). One of the largest examples of these cruder forms at present observed comes from Tell Halaf on the border of Syria, where a lion is shown playing on a tall narrow lyre with five strings (Pl. VIII, 1); the sound-chest is plain, there is no bull's head, and the whole reminds us of the Keltic *Chrotta* or *Rote* used in Northern Europe before the Christian era. From this it would appear that the Sumerians found the instrument already in use when they reached the Land of the Two Rivers. An Elamite seal shows a somewhat similar lyre with but four strings and no bull's head; on a potsherd (*c.* 2000) found at Larsa is displayed an eight-stringed instrument with short feet, but the "bull" form again is absent.

Unlike the bow-shaped harp, the lyre-type is not in any way characteristic of Central or Eastern Asia, but it was in use among the Subaraeans and the Semitic peoples, including Syrians, Phoenicians, Arabs and Hebrews, the last-named taking the lyre, called *kinnor*, as their national instrument and exhibiting it in later days on their coins.

In ancient Egypt of the XIIth Dynasty (*c.* 1950 B.C.) it is pictured in the hands of Semites at Beni-Hasan and was known to the Egyptians as the *kennarn-t*: on the other hand the large standing lyre, figured in the Egyptian wall-paintings at El Amarna (*c.* 1375 B.C.), finds no representative in Mesopotamia, though evidently of foreign introduction. We should therefore consider the lyre as more particularly the favourite of the Semitic-Akkadian population, but in later times improved and elaborated by their Sumerian neighbours. Undoubtedly the instruments discovered at Ur and dating from the early centuries of the third millennium B.C. show a remarkable advance on the primitive forms existing by their side. The sound-chest is most carefully constructed; sometimes it is covered with thin sheet silver affixed by little silver nails. It generally takes the shape of the sacred bull, its head projecting outwardly and decorated with gold, lapis lazuli and other adornments, while the narrow strip beneath the head is inlaid with shell mosaic, portraying the doings of national heroes and mythical beasts. Occasionally, as in the Lagash sculpture (Pl. VIII, 3), found at Tello and upon the stag lyre discovered at Ur (Pl. VII, 2), the animal is shown standing on the sound-chest in full relief. The oldest example of this bull-shaped lyre is given on a seal from Fâra, the ancient Sumerian Shuruppak on the Euphrates. It is of the Jemdet Nasr Period of the close of the fourth millennium B.C.; with its three strings, it is being played by an ass or perhaps a man so masked. These works of art provide moreover distinct evidence of detailed study from the musician's standpoint, as a reference to the illustrations here given will show: the curved "bout" in the sound-chest facilitates the action of the player's fingers; the setting of the bridge, the angle of the upright arms and the shape of the cross-bar (in some cases almost an "harmonic curve") all denote thoughtful design. But they are surpassed by the clever method adopted to ensure more accurate tuning of the strings, a device copied on the *citharae* of Greece and Rome and remaining still on the lyres of Abyssinia and Eastern Africa (Pl. VIII, 4). The device was as follows: on the cross-bar were placed small rods of wood or metal and the string, after being twisted round the bar, was affixed to the little rod: by raising or depressing one end of the rod, the tension of the string could be altered, the pitch being flattened or sharpened by this method for "fine tuning". These rods were found *in situ* on the silver lyre discovered at Ur (Pl. VII, 3) and are regularly shown in the seal impressions and mosaics (Pls. II, 1, 5; VIII, 2, 3), though it is noticeable that on the Agade (Semitic) seal on Plate II, 3 they are wanting. It may be that the little projections marked on the upper curve of the early Egyptian harps figured in the wall-paintings and generally called tuning "pegs" are in reality these same little tuning rods. The use of pegs was certainly of a much later date.

The number of strings on the large AL-GAR varies: eleven seems to have been a favourite arrangement, but instruments with five, six or eight strings are also shown in some instances. It has been suggested that this lyre was so heavy as to require more support than the player's strap would give: a seal impression (Pl. II, 5) is said to depict the instrument held up by two boys. We think this is very improbable, for the boys or dwarfs seem simply to be dancing with arms uplifted in front of the player. Before a seated performer the instrument was undoubtedly placed on the ground (Pls. II, 1; VIII, 2), but the representation of the lyrist and his singer on the royal standard shows how easily it could be suspended by a strap (Frontispiece).(6)

The lyre was employed especially as an accompaniment to the voice. In a hymn to Ishtar (*c.* 2100 B.C.) the poet says "I will speak to thee with the AL-GAR, whose sound is sweet"; and Gudea, at the appointment of his chief musician for the Lagash Temple, directs him "to banish the gloom of the city from the House of Comfort (the bridal chamber of Ningirsu and Baba) by the sound of the AL-GAR".

It was also used with other instruments in the dance (Pl. II, 5) but, unlike the upright harp, does not appear to have taken any prominent place in processions: in Egypt however it was constantly so carried.

In the temple ritual it had a definite place, for in Enki's Temple at Eridu we are told that "the holy AL-GAR sings in reverence". On the Abyssinian lyre (Pl. VIII, 4) there is inscribed in Ethiopic a thanksgiving for the help of the Trinity against the Gallas.(7)

Allusion has already been made to smaller instruments of the lyre type pictured on seals and in reliefs: many illustrations of these may be seen in Engel's *Music of the Most Ancient Nations* or in Lavignac's *Encyclopédie de la Musique*, Part I: some assume quite fantastic shapes, whilst others take us back to more primitive forms, such as those still to be found in Africa.

An instrument of this kind is named on the tablet last mentioned in praise of the Eridu Temple (*c.* 2200 B.C.) where it is called GIŠ SABÍTU, and also in a hymn to the Goddess Nanâ of later date (*c.* 720 B.C.) in which it is given the Assyrian equivalent *šebitu.*

Remembering the custom of these Oriental peoples in calling their instruments by names denoting the number of strings, this would be a "seven-stringed" lyre, similar to that shown on Plate **VI**, 7. The name SABÎTU (*šebitu*) corresponds to the Hebrew words *shibah* or *sheba,* Arabic *saba* ("seven"), the final syllable being the common Assyrian noun-ending. In certain dialects of Aramaic it appears as *shebᵉka* (*sabᵉka* in the Chaldee rendering of Daniel vi. 5), the hard guttural sound of the Hebrew final "a" (*ayin*) being emphasised. Here is the origin of the name of a small Phoenician lyre called *sabka* or *sabᵉka,* the *sambuke* of the Greeks and *sambuca* of the Romans. The instrument, as known in later days, appears to have varied in its size and number of strings, but it is described as being of triangular outline and like a boat with a ladder joined to it. The boat-shaped lyre (Pl. **VII**, 2) discovered at Ur answers in a peculiar manner to this description, and makes it clear why a military siege-engine, the *sambuca,* was named after it. The number of strings on this interesting specimen cannot be accurately ascertained, but it is evident that they were comparatively few; from traces left on the cross-bar probably seven. They were grouped together at one end of the sloping bar in order to avoid the figure of the stag which stands on the sound-chest. Some of the old illustrations of the ancient British *Crot* (*Rote*)—a small lyre—show the same shape as the SABÎTU.(8)

(c) THE LUTE

The idea of a stringed instrument with a small sound-box and a long neck, on which the strings could be "stopped" by the fingers, must have arisen from the hunting-bow through the primitive sound-producer known as the musical bow, which has been so ably described by Mr Henry Balfour. Here we can trace the long staff of the bow, the gourd-resonator attached to it and the use of the fingers on the string which at a later date, with a shorter neck and a larger body, became the Oriental and European lute. As has been stated already, the Indian *Vina,* especially in its northern form as the *Bîn,* is typical of the first steps in the development and history of this simple lute form. This primitive instrument appears in Mesopotamia early in the second millennium B.C. about the same time as it does in Egypt or perhaps a little earlier. It is said that in Egypt it was called *nefer,* meaning "good", and such a term might easily have been applied to so popular and useful an instrument: but the supposed derivation of the archaic hieroglyph from the instrument with its apparent tuning pegs is very unlikely, for, as Sir Flinders Petrie says, it more probably represents the lips, *trachea* and heart, from which "good things" should come. There are no traces of tuning pegs on these early lutes as there are none on the harps or lyres; the strings were simply twisted round the end of the neck, as in Africa to-day.

The Assyrian lute is evidently represented by the word ṢINNITU, found, in connection with other musical instruments, on an eighth-century tablet. It means the "two" strings, for so they are depicted with pendent ends on figurines from Kish and on Kassite seals of the second millennium B.C., as well as on Babylonian plaques of the same period. The instrument also appears in Hittite sculpture (c. 1000 B.C.), and at El Amarna (c. 1375 B.C.) it is pictured in close association with Syrian players. A terra-cotta plaque from Nippur, showing a shepherd performing on the ṢINNITU to his appreciative dog (Pl. VIII, 6), belongs to the Ist Babylonian Dynasty (c. 1900 B.C.) and, with its two strings, is a very early example. It was at first dated c. 2500 B.C., but erroneously.(9)

This long-necked lute, which later on had three or more strings, is widely known throughout the Nearer East as the *Tanbur*: but in earlier days its name seems to have been written *Pandur*, whence the Greek *Pandoura*. For the origin of this name we should like to suggest the following source: the *Tanbur* is called in Armenia *Pandir* and in Georgia *Panturi*. Now these countries were closely allied both by position and intercourse with Mesopotamia, and it has been ascertained that many Sumerian words for objects of common use were employed by these Eurasiatic hill-folk of mixed origin. In the Russian provinces of Asia evident traces of Sumerian tradition have been found. In Sumerian PAN-TUR means the "little bow". As we have already shown, the bow-shaped harp was originally called PAN throughout a wide district of Western Asia. The word TUR is still represented in the Georgian language by TAR, THIR or TUL which also mean "little", R and L being a common linguistic interchange. Indeed Pollux (*Onomasticon*) attributes the invention of the instrument to the Assyrians but, as it does not appear in their ritual use and is generally shown in the hands of peasants, mummers and dancers, it was probably of foreign extraction. In Al-Irāq it was especially popular during the opening centuries of our own era. Pythagoras (c. 540 B.C.) placed its origin in the Taurus.

A Babylonian boundary-stone (*kudurru*) of the Kassite Period (c. 1600 B.C.), now in the Louvre Museum, shows a representation of seven men with various creatures by their side—ostrich, panther, horse, ox, sheep, antelope and lion. The procession is led by a woman beating a timbrel and each of the men carries and plays a *Tanbur* (Pl. VIII, 7). It is supposed to depict the seven musicians from the Mesopotamian plain (GU-EDIN) bringing offerings to Ningirsu of Lagash, as described by Gudea on his cylinder.

This two-stringed lute is still found as a tribal instrument amongst the Kirghis and Kalmuck peoples near the Caspian Sea, and it survives in the national instrument of Russia, the *Balalaika*, originally with but two strings. Arab tradition attributes it to the men of Sodom and the Sabaeans; but as the Nabataeans at Palmyra are said to have used a very similar instrument, it probably came southward through the northern trade routes of which they were the masters in their day. The interchange of letters between Pandur and Tanbur follows a recognized rule.(10)

(d) THE PSALTERY

In conclusion there is one other instrument which, in the days of the Assyrian Empire, was certainly known, if not in general use. It is pictured on part of an ivory box, now in the British Museum, which was found in a palace at Nimrûd and is thought to be Phoenician work of about the ninth century B.C.

The subject is a procession of musicians with the double-pipe, timbrel and two rectangular instruments, which appear to be a kind of psaltery, an instrument with wire or gut strings stretched over a sound-chest. The strings, apparently eight in number, are being plucked with the fingers (Pl. VIII, 5).

It is not known when the psaltery type was first evolved, but in China the *Kin* and the *Tche*, both psalteries, have been in use from earliest times, at any rate from *c.* 2000 B.C.

In later centuries we find it square in shape instead of merely rectangular, and triangular or trapezoid forms are common. At the present day it is known in Turkey and India as the *Kanûn*, and in Arabia, Kurdistan, and Persia as the *Santir*, although it is, in this case, now usually struck as a dulcimer with two small sticks. Undoubtedly it is the *Pisanterin* mentioned in Daniel iii. 5 and translated "psaltery". In mediaeval Europe it was well known and frequently placed in the hands of angels by ecclesiastical artists and sculptors.

Its Sumerian and Akkadian name is very uncertain: but on a very late tablet of the Greek Period (*c.* 250 B.C.) containing a bilingual hymn in honour of Ishtar and written for her temple at Agade, we read "The musician (NAR) to my name [plays] on the SA-LI-NE-LU", which word in Akkadian is "*pagie*". SA-LI-NE-LU has been held by Dr Langdon (with a doubt) to mean "a bagpipe", but it appears more likely that it denotes an instrument with strings (SA), perhaps "many" strings. The noun *pagu* may imply that it was struck with a plectrum or the fingers by comparison with the Hebrew *paga*, "to strike" (*schlagen*—the technical word for playing with the fingers or a plectrum on the lute or mandoline). As regards its "many" strings we may recall the limitations of the artist with so small an object; but we must also recollect that on oriental instruments the strings are frequently arranged in sets of three or four, tuned in unison, and the artist may have endeavoured to represent this by the unusual thickness of the strings delineated. In some remote Russian villages a rectangular form of psaltery called the *gûsli* is still found with twenty-eight strings and in Sanskrit treatises (*c.* 200 B.C.) the *Katya-yana Vina* had its 100 strings! Probably one of the many thousands of tablets still undeciphered will one day reveal the name, in the same way as those already available have enabled us to provide the present provisional account of Sumerian musical instruments.(11)

Before closing this section, however, it may be well to repeat a caution which we gave twenty years ago in a note to the new edition of Stainer's *Music of the Bible*. Engel's "Assyrian dulcimer" described in his *Music of the Most Ancient Nations*, pp. 42 ff. is non-existent.

Although he admits that "the only representation is in too imperfect a state on the bas-relief to familiarise us intimately with its construction" and that "the slab appears to have been injured and slightly repaired afterwards, the defect extending over a portion of the dulcimer", yet, in his illustration, he fails to give the true state of affairs and has bequeathed to subsequent writers the laborious task of explaining this apparently unique instrument. A few years later Fétis in his *Histoire de la Musique* (I, p. 335) wrestled with the matter and suggested that the curved strings must have passed over pulleys and were weighted at the ends. Chappell followed and in his *History of Music* (p. 290) informs us that the instrument was fitted with curved metal rods fastened into a long shallow box as a sound-board: but it has been left to MM. Virolleaud and Pélagaud in Lavignac's *Encyclopédie de la Musique* (Part I, p. 46) to give us a detailed explanation and illustration of how such a thing could be, which is as surprising as it is ingenious. It is an attempt, say they, to represent in profile an instrument with a sound-board and thirteen (*sic*) strings which are stretched from hitch-pins over little studs and brought down to wrest-pins at the side of the case. "C'est à cette conception particulière de la perspective que nous devons cette étrange représentation qui a si bien dérouté ceux qui l'ont examinée."

For all this mental effort there is no need: a careful examination of the slab in the British Museum (No. 49) shows that at this point, of which we give a photographic reproduction (Pl. VI, 8), it has been cracked—as noted by Engel in 1864—at a weak part between a group of figures. The crack has passed down the little upright pillar of the triangular harp, practically obliterating it except just at the base and mutilating the strings on its outer side. These have been replaced in cement; but clumsily, as they fail to reach the height of the upper strings on the inner side. The repairer, however, shirked an attempt to make good the pillar itself: therefore the ten strings (as well as the subject) are left very much "in the air".

In reality it is a representation (and, when perfect, quite a good representation) of the familiar *Eširtu* or ten-stringed harp, already described and figured under this chapter.

CHAPTER IV

Scale and Notation

I N previous chapters we have been considering the instruments used by the Sumerians and those who immediately followed them in the Land of the Two Rivers. From the ancient tablets we have gathered, as far as is possible at present, their names and the uses to which they were put, a subject to which we shall revert in the next chapter. We have endeavoured to show their form and construction from extant examples dating from earliest times as well as from illustrations of them, lined either in the minute engravings of cylinder seals or in the larger and more detailed workmanship of bas-reliefs.

But we would go yet further: for the question naturally arises, Of what kind was the music which this wealth of instruments expressed?

To answer this we must deal first of all with the possibility of a definite scale or recognized succession of tones. We cannot imagine that so highly cultured a nation, as the Sumerians, would have been placidly content with a confused medley of heterogeneous sounds, when in other branches of art they showed so much method and achieved so great beauty.

(a) THE SCALE

Of making scales, or to use the German expression "sound-ladders", there seems, as of books, to be no end. They may be tetrachordic, pentatonic, heptatonic or, in their progression, diatonic, chromatic, enharmonic, etc.; but it is generally agreed that, in the first steps towards the development of this important branch in the art of music, the pentatonic or the heptatonic scales stand pre-eminent. It is necessary to emphasize this point because, in a very able paper read by Dr Curt Sachs before the Prussian Academy in 1924, a very elaborate system was attributed to these ancient Mesopotamian peoples. Of this however we shall speak in the next section of the chapter.[1]

The first real scale formed by man has generally been supposed to have been pentatonic, a theory much pressed in our own country by Engel and Chappell in their histories of early music. But it is now realized that although a five-note system is widely circulated amongst primitive races found in Eastern Africa, the southern parts of Asia and in Indonesia (known as the Erythrean culture), yet other cultures have from the earliest times had a heptatonic or seven-note scale. This is particularly true of a nation which has usually been upheld as a champion of the pentatonic system—the Chinese. It may be, that before the Chinese migrated from Western or Central Asia to the eastern coast, the aboriginal inhabitants of the latter region had the Erythrean culture of their immediate neighbours. But a famous Chinese antiquary of the imperial house, Prince

Tsai-yü, who lived in the sixteenth century, vigorously combated the idea, prevalent in his own day, that his national scale was originally pentatonic. "If [he writes] our scholars had a little less assurance and a little more knowledge, it would often save them from making certain mistakes, which render them contemptible in the eyes of those who understand these subjects." Then he proceeds to show, by quotations from ancient Chinese authors, that, from the most distant days of antiquity, their scale had seven recognized sounds. The origin of the present "official" five-note scale (for the popular instruments still possess the seven-note) is due to an edict issued in the Ming Dynasty (fifteenth century A.D.), which excluded all semitones and so obviated the difficulty which the Chinese musicians found in expressing that interval properly—a difficulty not unknown in our own day. Tsai-yü moreover tells us that he had himself seen a genuine specimen of an ancient Chinese vertical flute in bronze, called YO or TI (Pl. XI, 1); it dated from before the Chou Dynasty (c. 1122 B.C.). He gives—true antiquary as he was—careful measurements of every detail and also directions for producing the scale: it was heptatonic. The instrument had but three holes for the fingers, placed equidistantly, but by the use of the harmonics the natural series of sounds obtainable, as we have proved by an exact reproduction, are as follows:

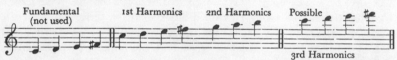

For convenience of reference the actual pitch has been transposed a tone lower. Now we have seen that the vertical flute used by the Sumerians was called TI-GI (Akkad. *tigu* or *tegu*), and the Chinese historians say that the word or name TI (of which the old pronunciation was more like TIK or TEK) had a connection with the Ch'iang people, a tribe living to the west of the Chinese border. It was evidently an early importation and Professor Moule, to whose intimate knowledge of Chinese music we are greatly indebted, has pointed out that the Chinese character, still in use (Pl. X, 4), was most probably derived from the original form of this three-holed flute itself. We are also told by Tsai-yü that the ancients thought very highly of the YO or TI (both originally *vertical* flutes identical save in length and perhaps slightly in embouchure) "because they had therein the principles which had served the first authorities in fixing the sounds of the *lüs*" There is no need to enter here into the traditional origin of these *lüs* or pitch-pipes for the Chinese semitonal progressions: placing on one side the fantastic accounts which have been handed down to us, it seems that the Imperial Minister Ling Lun ("Master of Music") sent by Huang-ti in the third millennium B.C. westward, over the K'unlun Mountains "to study its proper ordering", came across

a people in Western Asia, some say in Bactria, whose musical scale he adopted
and cut his bamboo or reed tubes to accord with the notes he had heard—a wise
precaution. On his return to the Emperor with his pitch-pipes, the scientists
proceeded to develop the scheme of successive fifths and fourths, which became
the mathematical explanation of this western scale and was enshrined in the
twelve *lüs*, of which, however, seven sounds noted by their Minister were held
to be the chief.(2)

Unfortunately, owing to the perishable nature of the material generally used
for these simple flutes, we have no actual specimen of the Sumerian instrument;
but it is shown on the archaic seal in the Louvre (Pl. IV, 1) and on the seal
impression from Ur, already mentioned and illustrated on Plate II, 5; the player
is here seen holding his flute in the same way as the ancient Chinese TI: it is
moreover similar in length and apparently, from the position of the fingers,
possesses but three holes. We know too that the instrument also bore the name
IMIN-E or "the seven-note" corresponding to Tsai-yü's scale. The Sumerian
word E, which literally means "voice", reminds us also of the "hepta phoneenta"
or "seven voices" of the flute used by the Egyptian priests to hymn their gods,
as described by Demetrius Phalereus (*c.* 317 B.C.), and the "septem discrimina
vocum" of the Thracian lyre. Fortunately too there were discovered at Beni
Hasan, by Dr Garstang, two long Egyptian flutes made of reed, and dating from
the Middle Empire (*c.* 2000 B.C.). From exact reproductions made of them we
find that they possess a similar scale (derived in the same way harmonically),
but, of course, of deeper pitch, as the flutes are a yard or more in length (Pl. XI, 2).
Thus the scale at this early period in Egypt appears to have been identical with
that used in Western Asia and in China—viz. a diatonic progression with an
augmented (or tritone) fourth. On the long Egyptian flutes this fact is particularly noticeable as, owing to the wide stretch of the fingers required to cover the
three holes, it would have eased the player if the uppermost hole had been placed
nearer the middle hole. But, instead of that, we find that the middle hole is
brought up close to the uppermost hole for the simple reason that the latter was
required to produce the equivalent of F sharp and not of F natural, whereas the
pitch of the middle hole could be flattened by closing the lowest hole. Moreover,
according to Dr Cohen, the oldest vocal traditions of the Jewish Synagogue are
enshrined in the *Neginoth*—accentual cantillations of Scripture—preserved with
greatest purity by the Jews of Northern Europe and said to have been handed
down from the days of Ezra (fifth century B.C.). Here, in the official manual,
we note that at the reading of the Prophets this tritone scale is employed; only in
an occasional passing-note is the fourth treated as if perfect. All this points to
the existence of such a particular seven-note scale over a wide area, at any rate
in Asia, and its special characteristic—the tritone—explains a difficulty which

has also embarrassed students of Indian music: for instance, Mr Fox Strangways in his *Music of Hindostan* (1914) writes "there is no accounting for this—the appearance of the tritone—it must be accepted as a fact: it is a fundamental part of Indian music"; but there is no difficulty if the ancient Indian seven-note scale contained it also. Old Corean melodies show the same interval.

It is interesting too to observe that on the south-eastern coast of Arabia, so closely connected in bygone days with Sumerian and probably Indian trade, the like scale is found. Thus a specimen of a native chant, as given by Mr Bertram Thomas in his *Arabia Felix* (1932), is as follows, transposed however for comparison to a lower pitch:

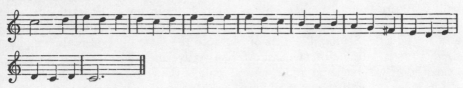

Among the Bantu tribes of Africa the three-hole flute and the same heptatonic scale are prevalent.(3)

Apart however from the vertical flutes, this theory of the old Asiatic diatonic scale, as borne out by the ancient instruments that have been discovered, requires careful consideration. The slender reed-pipes are capricious and very difficult to test, for so much depends on the size and strength of the reed employed, and of this no usable example has been preserved. We have nevertheless experimented with exact reproductions of the two Ur pipes mentioned in Chapter II and illustrated on Plate IV, 3, and, by the aid of a small beating-reed used on the Syrian *Meijiwis* (*Zummârah*), have obtained the following scale, of which further details are given in the notes to this chapter.(4)

Fundamental   1st Harm.

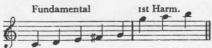

If we look, again, to the stringed instruments, they of course can be tuned to any progression; and here too artists and sculptors often omitted strings, if space were limited. We can only, therefore, consider proofs afforded by actual specimens or by names denoting a certain number of strings: we may, for instance, quote the Akkadian *SABÍTU* with its "seven strings" and the *EŠIRTU* or "ten-stringed" harp ($1\frac{1}{4}$ octave); the ZAG-SAL or "cross-strung" harp, found in two forms, one with eleven strings ($1\frac{1}{2}$ octave)—a general compass too for the large AL-GAR or lyre in contemporary illustrations—and the other with fifteen strings (2 octaves).

In the Louvre and the Musikinstrumenten-Museum at Berlin there are Egyptian specimens of the ZAKKAL or upright harp with twenty-one strings (Pl. **VI**, 1, 2), i.e. three series of seven-note scales after the Chinese system; while on a bas-relief a fourteen-stringed instrument suggests a two series combination.

The small lyres held by captives or by nomads have generally but five strings: on the Bismyan vase (*c.* 3000) the bow-shaped harps have seven and five strings respectively (the latter instrument being cramped for want of space). The large lyre, held by the ass in the Ur inlay, and the Larsa lyre, have eight strings (octave): the Assyrian "trigons" show sometimes nine strings, corresponding to the Mongol use of an octave and a tone; but, as already said, uncertainty prevails in illustrations. Another point of interest lies in the fact that this tritone diatonic scale was in use amongst the Russian Finns in the eighteenth century; and amongst the Southern Berbers of Morocco the same interval is also emphasized, as it is in some of the East African native melodies, while an instance nearer home will be found in the natural scale of the Highland bagpipe chanter.

The lowering of this augmented fourth was due to various causes: in the Greek tetrachord system it had no place: to the Gregorian singers it was very *diabolus* himself. In China, the fourteenth century of our era saw it eclipsed by the perfect fourth of the Mongol invaders.(5)

Nevertheless the Sumerians must have had much fair music in their day: after all, it is a question of intonation on the part of the performer and of appreciation, fortified by usage, on the part of the listener. Let us also recognize that the scale of their three-holed flute was more true than it became in later days, when the six-holed or seven-holed instrument was introduced: it was harmonically correct. The fact that the series consists of twenty-one sounds instead of twenty-two and is not completed by a final octave note may also appear peculiar and, to our ears, unsatisfactory; but a "tritone" scale does not demand such completion; for the sharpened fourth emphasizes the fifth (or dominant), around which the melody is grouped, irrespective of the so-called key-note or tonic.

(b) NOTATION

Following on the fixing of the scale there would naturally arise, in course of time, a desire to express by means of writing the various sounds of voices and instruments. This "notation", as we call it, is so commonplace a thing with us that we can hardly realize the length of years which elapsed before such a simple method, as we possess, was achieved.

It is to the Greeks we have hitherto looked for the earliest efforts in this direction, for they made use of the letters of the alphabet, as the Hindoos had done before them; the Persians meanwhile employed numbers.

Now it is generally recognized that a notation for instruments preceded that for voices. The earliest western form was the application of an old Dorian alphabet, showing traces of Phoenician or Semitic origin, to the notes of a sixteen-stringed lyre or harp, embracing a two-octave diatonic system with an added note. The Hindoos, on the other hand, confined their notation, consisting of five consonants and two vowels, to the intervals of their seven-note scale.(6)

Whether the Egyptians possessed some method of writing down their music is not at present known, but the interesting question before us at the moment is whether the Sumerians or their compatriots, the Akkadians, had not already discovered the possibility of so doing centuries before the Greeks evolved their recognized systems.

We must now allude to a very remarkable tablet known as KAR I, 4 and preserved in the Staatliches Museum, Berlin, of which we give a photograph on Plate IX, showing both sides. In 1915 it was deciphered and translated by Dr Ebeling and presents to us in its central column a Sumerian Hymn on the Creation of Man. It was found at Asshur and is dated c. 800 B.C. The hymn is furnished with an Assyrian translation in the right-hand column and in the left-hand column there are certain groups of cuneiform signs which seem to indicate the music. It was on the strength of these that Dr Curt Sachs attributed to the old inhabitants of Mesopotamia a very intricate scale formation. He has stated that the Babylonians, in a wide sense of the word, had a non-chromatic pentatonic musical system but that their melodies were not bound to one rigid five-tone scale; they could range freely within four inter-related five-tone scales. There were in fact chromatic and enharmonic alternatives.

Here surely Dr Sachs is reading into the interpretation of the signs features of a much later date, more consonant with the dictates of Aristoxenus as expressed in the Greek system of the fourth century B.C.

Moreover, since his paper was written, other traces of these same signs have been found at Sippar near Babylon which carry them back to at least the sixteenth century B.C. Professor Landsberger, therefore, in the *Freiherr von Oppenheim Festschrift* (1933) definitely states that Sach's interpretation is pure assumption, because Babylonian culture never attained to so high a pitch. He considers that the meaning of these signs is now past finding out, even though later Assyrian scribes tried to translate them in the syllabaries. With this conclusion we cannot agree; though, as Wilkinson has remarked of the ancient Egyptians, any method of preserving melodies by a notation would have been concealed by the priests with the same jealous care as the mysteries themselves. Impossible? If that is all, as Cobden said, we had better set about it at once.

Now it has been suggested that these detached signs were found useful as writing copies and exercises for the scholars at the great Sippar School attached to the temple, for they are there found isolated from the hymn and appear to have served some such purpose. But an examination of their character and arrangement precludes the idea that this was their original intention. Many of the simplest cuneiform signs are repeated again and again—the sign for A, for instance, thirty-one times in seventy-one lines; whilst the more difficult are rarely written more than twice—an inversion of the usual scholastic methods.(7)

But it may be asked, Why are the signs repeated at all in the face of the vast number a student of literature had to master? The only answer is that they must denote something more than mere syllables or letters: they represent sounds: and here we are in agreement with Dr Sachs—the sounds of the harp. If they had been the notation for a w'nd instrument (flute or pipe), there would have been no need to repeat a sign five times successively in a single line. But the strings of the harp were not sufficiently resonant to continue the required accompaniment to the chanter's voice and the player had to pluck his string again and again, as on the ancient Chinese psalteries.

Now these signs, as in all old cuneiform writing, are not really letters, except in one or two instances: they are syllables, and, owing to the primitive character of the Sumerian language, they can express various cognate ideas connected with the original pictographs from which they were taken: nay more, they can have more than one phonetic value or pronunciation. For instance, the sign BAD may be read as uš, MIT, PIT, SUN, ZI, or TIL, with varying derived meanings: and, as Mr Gadd points out in his *Sumerian Reading Book*, the true reading of such a sign in any given passage "must, in the last resort, depend upon the context".

Here, in these detached signs of the tablet, the only context is the line of the hymn against which they are placed, and we have come to the conclusion that the correct reading was conveyed to the musician by his knowledge of the context of the hymn.

We first noticed this in dealing with the fourteenth line of the tablet (obverse), which tells of "the rivers Tigris and Euphrates": against this line is placed a sign which can be read as NUN or as ZIL, but as NUN is applied with special reference to their "*Great* River" Euphrates (BURA-NUN), it was evidently intended to be read so. In the reference notes to this chapter a further and fuller illustration of this process has been given, and by working through each sign in this way we have been able to express their intended values. By no other method can this be done and its importance will be apparent when we come to speak of them as "notation" signs. Some of the references they bear to the text of the hymn are amusingly plain: others are more difficult; but these difficulties would not occur for those who used them in the days when Sumerian was a living language.(8)

Recalling that the earliest notation systems at present known were based on alphabetical lines, the proposition to be solved in the present instance is how a syllabic sign could be applied to an alphabetical series. This has always been done by the powerful principle of acrophony, whereby the initial sound of the syllable is used to express a letter. We ourselves used it in our earliest days when, learning our English alphabet, we were told that "A is for Ape, B for Bear, M for Man, N for Nag" and so on, although it was not quite in accordance with more modern ideas of tuition.

Now an ordered series of letters was already in existence: for not only had the Egyptians evolved an acrophonic alphabet from their hieroglyphics, but in Mesopotamia the knowledge of an early Aramaic (North Semitic) alphabet was general in the second millennium B.C., a fact which is being confirmed by striking and recent discoveries, as at Sinai, Ras Shamra and Lachish.

It would appear that a musical scribe or priest of some Mesopotamian temple who was conversant with Semitic, perhaps his mother-tongue, applied the sounds of the cuneiform syllabic signs acrophonically to the ordered arrangement of this Semitic alphabet; Professor Landsberger also calls the signs a *Silbenalphabet*. So he evolved a notation which denoted the note of each string of the large upright harp (*ZAKKAL*) which, to judge from the many figurines of harpists discovered at Sippar (Pl. VI, 6), was in general use at Babylon in the opening centuries of the second millennium.(9)

There are twenty-one letters for its twenty-one strings, the number shown on the bas-reliefs of Assyria and on actual specimens preserved at Paris and Berlin (Pl. VI, 1, 2). These letters represent the twenty-one recognized sounds used in Sumerian as expressed by the phonetic values of the signs, viz. the vowels *a, e, i, u* and the consonants *b, d, g, ḫ, k, ḳ, l, m, n, p, r, s, ṣ, š, t, ṭ, z.* In adapting them to the order of his Semitic alphabet, the scribe had to omit the Semitic aspirate *h* (Heb. *he*) which did not exist in Sumerian. He had also to employ the weak consonants (*aleph, waw* and *yod*) and the lighter-voiced *ayin* to represent the Sumerian vowel sounds, a common practice in the Semitic languages themselves. "It has been held", writes Mr Gadd in his *Reading Book,* "that the consonants *ḳ (q), ṣ (ts or z)* and *ṭ (rough t)* did not exist in Sumerian; but, as the signs which involve these sounds are constantly used in their writings, it is difficult to account for their presence if they did not correspond with a real necessity of the language." In Akkadian and Assyrian cuneiform they are abundantly present.

Thus the musician was provided with a definite series of letter-signs adapted to the compass of his instrument. It may, of course, have been a unique experiment, a method of fixing the inflections of the chanter's voice for this particular hymn or series of hymns. We hope, however, that other instances will be recovered; but at present we must express our belated thanks to the scribe of the ninth century B.C. who, having found the detached signs on one tablet, attached them once more to the words of the hymn, which he had discovered on another tablet. To him these signs must have conveyed some particular meaning for each line of the hymn. His hymn tablet was imperfect: he tells us so. But he has placed his notation signs against the empty lines marked "missing" (*ḫiepi*) in order that the correct signs should appear with the proper words when the text of the hymn was resumed. We think that he made one slight slip and that, according to the notation-sign readings, line 54 (reverse 13) should occupy in the text two lines instead of one, and that lines 63, 64 (reverse 23, 24) should run as one. We have so arranged them in the transcript, wherein we have also boldly attempted to restore the sense of the missing words of lines 44–6 (reverse 3–5) from the meaning indicated by the notation-signs, placing such restoration within brackets. We considered that some words, at any rate, were necessary for the due rendering of the hymn. Taking then these twenty-one acrophonic letter-signs for the twenty-one strings of the harp and giving them their names in the Hebrew form, which is nearest akin to the old northern Semitic dialect, they are as follows, the corresponding sounds in ordinary Roman letters being placed below them:

Aleph	Beth	Gimel	Daleth	Waw	Zain	Kheth	Ṭet	Yod	Kəph	Lamed
a	b	g	d	u	z	ḫ (kh)	ṭ	i	k	l

Mem	Nun	Samech	Ayin	Pe	Tsade	Qoph	Resh	Shin	Tau
m	n	s	e	p	ṣ (ts)	ḳ (q)	r	š (sh)	t

As ancient melodies generally descend in sound-pitch at their close, we may well consider "a" as representing the longest string and so the deepest sound. But what sound? Here we turn to the flute scale explained in the first section of this chapter. Like the completed Chinese seven-note scale, it appears on the twenty-one stringed Mesopotamian harp in three diatonic series—low, medium and high—each with its "tritone" fourth. As regards pitch, from a comparison of the large upright harp with the average height of the Assyrian musicians delineated on the bas-reliefs, we should be warranted, as we have said, in fixing its lowest note at D, or at C—two lines below our bass stave, the string for that note on a mediaeval harp being about three feet in length, which is also the length of the longest string on the Louvre and Berlin upright harps. The scale, compass and notation are therefore as follows:

In order to elucidate this method of transcription yet further, we append the first eight lines of notation signs in the hymn:

—Me (g) Me (g) Pa (d¹) Pa (d¹) → —Me(g) Me(g) Pa(d^1) Pa(d^1)

—A (C) A (C) A (C) A (C) A (C)

—Ku (e) Ku (e) Dib (F♯) Dib (F♯)

—Maš (g) Maš (g) Maš (g)

—Maš (g) Zal (A) Maš (g) Zal (A)

—Si (b) Zal (A) Si (b) Zal (A) Si (b) A (C)

—U (G) Bar (D) Bar (D) Bar (D)

—Lal (f♯) Lal (f♯) Igi (d) Bar (D)

In the right-hand column the reading of the sign is given; the capital letter denotes the acrophonic value; the letters in brackets show the relative pitch according to the scale already set out. The older or Sippar text is followed, though in these lines there is no difference between it and the later Ninevite copy, except that for DIB a more archaic Babylonian form of the sign is used, as we should naturally expect in the earlier centuries of the second millennium. Mr Gadd observes that the first three signs are reminiscent of infantile attempts at human speech—a not inappropriate beginning for a Hymn on Man's Creation. An explanation of the way in which the correct reading of these notation signs is correlated with the sentiments expressed in the respective lines of the poem opposite to them will be found in Note 8 to this chapter. In the notation the chanter's voice-part is, of course, missing, but we are led to consider from the statement of many ancient writers, including Plato and Aristotle in the fourth century B.C., as well as by the usual custom of Oriental peoples, that the accompaniment was in octaves to the voice, when not actually in unison with it. Perhaps, in later days, a fifth or a fourth might have been added by the instrumentalist to strengthen the emphasis, as was the unwritten practice on the Chinese psalteries; but we find no trace of harmony in the notation. In the full score of the hymn, which will be found at the end of the Notes on the Chapters (p. 99), we have therefore ventured to restore the voice-part on these lines, taking it through a normal compass of ten notes as found on the companion instrument, the EŠIRTU. It must be remembered that the hymn was chanted in *quasi-recitativo* form and the notation, as given in crotchets, merely denotes *stress*, the singer choosing such time and rhythm as would best suit the words, and the supporting harpist plucking his strings accordingly. No bars are shown on the music-lines, the small numbers placed above represent the successive lines of the hymn, and the instrumental part below denotes the number of notes played during each such line. The Sumerian words are given, as normally most suited to the music set for them—the pronunciation is *more Italiano* and the letter *ḫ* is sounded as "*kh*", and the letter *š* as "*sh*". An English version is also added for the purpose of showing the way in which the instrument, in the phrase of an old Greek writer, added to "the due modulation and expression of the words". Upon the subject of the structure of the hymn, however, more will be said in the next chapter, which deals with the Appreciation of Music.(10)

Beneath the harpist's stave is given, on a single line, the syllabic notation used acrophonically by the original Sumerian scribe. It is based, by preference, on the Sippar text as being the oldest and simplest: the version employed by the copyist of the Assyrian period has evidently suffered from later attempts at elaboration. He has however added at the foot of the tablet the following note, for no doubt he realized how difficult the explanation would be to some future enquirer. In it he has adopted the priestly attitude of even later days:

> "*Pirištu mudû mudâ lukalim.*"
> "The secret let the learned reveal to the learned."

Has the secret perished with him, or are we still too unlettered to deserve it?

The following free translation of the hymn will perhaps afford some idea of its stateliness and beauty: the lines have been arranged to accord with the revised original.

A HYMN ON THE CREATION OF MAN

When heav'n and earth, the constant pair, were fram'd,
Divine Inanna, Mother Goddess, form'd;
When in the place ordain'd the earth was laid
And heav'n therewith in harmony design'd;
When, straight as line, stream and canal flow'd on   5
And Tigris and Euphrates fill'd their banks;
Then An and Enlil, Utu and Enki,
  Gods almighty,
With the great gods, the Anunnaki,
Sat in their high abode majestical,   10
And one to other thus address'd their words.
"Now that the bounds of heav'n and earth are fix'd
And, lin'd upon their course, stream and canal,
Broad Tigris' flood and great Euphrates' roll,
Each pent within its own appointed bed;   15

Can more by us be done?
What else be made?
O Anunnaki, Gods of earth supreme,
What would ye now?
What ask us more to do?"   20
Whereto the Gods of earth, all standing by,
The Anunnaki, in whose hands is fate,
Two to Enlil omnipotent replied:
"Where heav'n and earth do meet on Uzuma
Both craftsman-gods together ye shall slay,   25
And of their blood Mankind shall ye create.
On them the service of the Gods enjoin,
The border stream to tend
With diligence,
Their hands with spade and basket   30
To employ,
The mansion of the Gods
To magnify,
The fields, enclos'd within their measur'd bounds,
Th'engirdling stream to hold   35
Inviolate,
The channel course and stone
To keep untouch'd,
The tilth to water, plants to fruit
Mature;   40
The very heav'ns [with fav'ring eyes look down]
As thus they open forth earth's inwardness,
And storied lofts with harvest reapings fill,
[With treasures too, borne far on wave and way;
While plenteousness attends each hearth and home   45
And all the country smiles in sweet accord:]
Thus shall the Anunnaki fields abound,
Fair increase in the land augment their weal,
The festivals divine be duly kept
With fresh libations of pure water pour'd,   50
Where high the temple of the Gods doth stand.
Emblazon'd 'Lords of Plenty' as their meed,
'Masters of Riches', very Gods themselves,
Their oxen, cattle,
Sheep, and fish and bird   55
Throughout the land shall in abundance dwell,
As to the Gods Enul and Ereshul
Loud praises rise aloft from purest lips."
Thou, blest Aruru, Goddess Queen of all,
Shalt for their sons high destinies allot;   60
Men wise in letters, brave in deeds, shall rise

Like ears of corn, self-springing from the ground,
While, fix'd in their eternal seats, the stars
Revolve the round of holy feast and fast.
    This, of their own unfetter'd will, the Gods   65
        Have so decreed:
        By An and by Enlil,
        By Enki and Ninmakh,
        Almighty Gods.
Here too, where men first drew their living breath,   70
All-bounteous Nisaba hath set her sway.

CHAPTER V

The Appreciation of Music

FROM all that has been hitherto said, it will be gathered that the foundations of music and of the various methods of expressing it had been well and truly laid in the Land of Sumer when the curtain rises on the earliest historic scene. But, in order that we may appreciate the genius of this remarkable people, it will be well for us to obtain some idea of the ways in which their musical art was employed and the purposes which it was made to serve. In fact, we must try to inhale some waft of the musical atmosphere of this land and breathe its native air.

Now it is very evident that the centre around which music revolved was worship. The frequent allusions to it and the various directions, given in our previous quotations, concerning it are almost wholly connected with the rituals and ceremonies of the temple. Perhaps however it may be well not to lay too great a stress upon this point, because in those early days, as indeed in our own mediaeval times, the knowledge of writing and the recording of history were largely in the hands of the priestly order. The schools of instruction attached to the temples lead very definitely to the conclusion that learning was the monopoly of the few, and they of a particular class set apart to deal with religious rites rather than with popular customs and everyday doings. In this respect we are not in so favourable a position as regards the Sumerians as we are with the ancient Egyptians. For, while the impressions of the Mesopotamian seals, especially in the earlier period, depict musical subjects, they are almost always of a religious or semi-religious character; whereas the early tomb-paintings of Egypt reveal domestic scenes and admit us to the ordinary occupations of the people.

We may say indeed that, until we come to the age of the Assyrian bas-reliefs in the first half of the first millennium B.C., we are seldom permitted to mark how music played its part in the wider area of the state. The exceptions which do occur (and they are given us from the archaic period) are connected rather with the pastoral life of the people. We see the flute-playing shepherd (Pl. IV, 1) charming, like a later Orpheus, his flocks and his dog: or, in centuries more recent, herdsmen leading in marked submission the wild animals of the desert or the domesticated creatures of the country-side to the strains of the long-necked lute (Pl. VIII, 6). On the other hand, as in the famous royal standard of Ur, we are admitted to the banquet of the king and his nobles (Frontispiece) to share with them the vocal accomplishments of the trained singer attuning her voice to the strains of the lyre, which in the inscription of Gudea are said "to drive away the gloom of the city". Perhaps too the small monkey seated beneath a spreading tree and sounding his little reed-pipe (Pl. II, 2) suggests a bucolic scene. But these musically-gifted animals, of which we speak more fully below, and which are frequently represented in the early seals and on such inlay as that on the royal harp of Ur, are closely connected with nature mythology and may be more properly referred to fable than to fact. Certainly the scene depicted in the lower register of one of Queen Shubad's seals appears to portray a feast given by the Queen to her immediate friends, to which her harpist and tambourine player, together with two vocalists, are summoned (Pl. II, 4). All these representations are very different in character to those sculptured in the Assyrian palaces of the ninth to the seventh centuries B.C., where music is made the background to the blood-stained triumphs of mighty kings and the orgies of merciless rulers.

In dealing, however, with the temple music we have every assistance given us by the tablets, which contain explicit directions for the due performance of rites and ceremonies, as well as by the many inscriptions which record the gifts of governors and monarchs. For, at any rate in the earlier periods, the hope and consolation of the Sumerian soul revolved around the temple, which, with its lofty terraced tower, dominated the city life. It has been remarked by several writers that the outlook of this gifted people towards a future existence was very shadowy, almost gloomy: "to-day" was all they could call their own and that was cursed and hampered by ill-luck, disease and distress. To ward off the demons, who were the cause of all this misfortune, was the aim of the layman and, for this end, he seems to have had a lingering form of serpent worship or propitiation; for to him the serpent was the symbol of all evil and harm. But, as his efforts in this direction proved unavailing, he looked to the official ritual for the relief he sought. There was an organized system of incantation, exorcism and libations, and he laid it to the duty of the priest. Hence all that was connected with the temple was to him "life" compared to the surrounding "death". Perhaps this sentiment explains some of the attributes credited to the musical instruments used in the services—the flute TI-GI seems to mean "the reed of life", the sound of the copper kettledrum in the open forecourt, as it reverberated through the streets of the city, was a "living sound", while the temple itself was known as "The House of Life" (E-NAM-TI-LA). Did not there stand within its walls the Sacred Tree, emblem of life and fertility!

In connection then with this central fountain of hope Dr Langdon, in the introduction to his work on the Babylonian Liturgies, has provided us with many interesting facts: from these we can gain some idea of the organization of the temple services and, from other sources, gather a general knowledge of the lay-out of the various courts and buildings in which such important ceremonies took place.

The usual plan of a Sumerian temple consisted of a sacred enclosure of rectangular shape, within which were the necessary buildings with their forecourt, all raised on a substantial platform. Into the court the worshipper passed through a pillared gateway and in it the principal rites were celebrated and sacrifices offered. The temple proper or the shrine of the god was originally a simple reed-hut, a relic of primitive days; but early in historic times it was built of more durable materials: around it were grouped chambers for the preparation and performance of the required services. The immediate precincts also contained dwelling-rooms for the priests and their attendants, storehouses, granaries, a good cellar of wine and a sacred well. The most prominent object, however, though not necessarily the oldest, was the temple tower or *ziggurat*, which rose in four to eight stages and was crowned, according to Herodotus, by a small room or chapel, empty save for a gold bed and a gold table. Here, in the meeting-place of earth and heaven, the chosen priestess by night received the revelation of the god.

The oracle, thus given, was delivered by a priest to the strains of the "cross-strung" harp (ZAG-SAL) or of the lyre (AL-GAR), a custom continued by the Hebrew prophets and psalmists, who "opened their dark sayings upon the harp".

Of priests there were various orders: the high priest (SANGA-MAḤ) was in the earliest period the king of the city or the governor (IŠAG); as such he was the earthly representative of the deity; it was only in later days that he became the god himself. Under his direction the SANGU-priests were permitted to handle the sacred objects and to exercise their office in divination and exorcism.

The musical establishment consisted of liturgists and psalmists, who were charged with the proper conduct of the daily services and their ordered chanting. In the great temple of Ningirsu at Lagash, so splendidly restored and equipped by the King-priest Gudea *c.* 2400 B.C., they were under the direction of a special officer, who was responsible for their training: with him was associated another official, who was in charge of the choir. The chanters and musicians, who included both male and female performers, were grouped under several titles which are difficult to define exactly: but, as a rule, the NAR (Akkadian *naru*, if feminine, *nartu*) was a musician, that is, a performer on the flute, double-pipe, harp, lyre or drum, or, perhaps, a singer to some such accompaniment: while the UŠ-KU, LAGAR or GALA was a liturgical psalmist or chanter. In Akkadian the former appears to have been also called *zammeru* (if feminine, *zammiertu*) and the latter *kalu*, but the names are much interchanged. The GALA or *kalu* certainly accompanied himself on the sacred drum (BALAG), for the Gudea statue records in its inscription that, such was the happy lot of that time, "in the cemetery of the city no corpse was buried, the psalmist (GALA) brought not his drum and wailing went not up": probably it was more a question of ecclesiastical rank than of actual duty. In the early period the GALA, it appears, was not a consecrated priest: he sang to win the favour of the gods. In a hymn of lamentation over the desolation of the land we read:

> O temple, thy skilled master is not present; thy fate who decrees?
> The psalmist, who knows the song, is not present; thy fate to the drum he chants not!
> He that knows how to touch the drum is not present, thy fate he sings not!

There seem to have been various grades amongst them, for the chief psalmist (UŠ-KU MAḤ) was a permanent official of the temple with a high salary, whereas other psalmists were engaged in ordinary business, assisting only on special occasions. Their education, however, must have been generally thorough and wide, for an Assyrian scribe describes the GALA or *kalu* as "the Wisdom of Ea", God of Letters. In the forecourt of the temple the large drum (A-LA) was "set up" and—if our correlation be correct—in some places a large bell (NIG-KAL-ЗA). Here certain ceremonies of libation and supplication were performed; in the great temple at Lagash and probably also at Eridu they were accompanied by the blowing of horns. Hither too were brought the sacred drum (BALAG) and the ritual flute (TI-GI) to swell the strains of the grand music, though it is a question, owing to the restricted size of the forecourt, whether public worship, as we know it, was possible.

Within the temple were the stringed instuments used for accompanying the psalmists and chanters; they included the harp (AL or ZAG-SAL), which the scribe of a Nippur tablet especially attributes to Enlil. It was played during the oracular utterances of the high-priest: hence it was called "the instrument of the decision of fate" and "by day and by night its sound was heard". Sometimes it was combined with the ritual flute and, in a late record, it leads an orchestra composed of the seven-stringed lyre (*šebitu*), the "covered" pipe (*kanzabu*), the single-pipe of oboe type (*malilu*), the two-stringed lute (*sinnitu*) and "other instruments". Whether it was employed for processional purposes outside the temple is an open question: its large size and shape must have rendered it awkward to carry, although on Plate V, 4, 5, we find it held in the arms; but the elaborate bow-shaped harps of Egypt were either placed on the ground or rested on a stand: there was, however, in Mesopotamia the smaller form, called *mirîtu*, which was portable and more like the original type: it is seen in the hands of a woman (Pl. II, 4). The lyre (AL-GAR) appears to have superseded the large harp in certain temples, as at Lagash, where instructions were given by Gudea to the chief musician, who played the sacred drum, bidding him cultivate diligently flute-playing and the use of the lyre, although Dr Langdon's reading of the passage would add also the *mirîtu* or small bow-shaped harp just mentioned.

At Eridu it was called "the Holy AL-GAR of Enki" or Ea, God of Music as well as of Letters, and with the seven-note flute was used in hymns of penitence and adoration. In incantations too the drum, the lyre and the flute appear to have been combined: its counterpart, the Hebrew *kinnor*, was employed in accompanying prophecy and exorcism, bringing refreshment to the distracted Saul and vision of the future to the inspired psalmist. Its presence at the laments for the dead may be inferred from the statue-inscription which describes the golden age of Gudea, when sorrow was unknown and in the temple cemetery "no lyre sounded": if so, it would anticipate the use of this instrument in the Greek *threnoi* or dirges, in the Hebrew wailings and in the Irish chanting of the *cepog* to their *cruit*, which was more like a lyre than a harp and known also as the Chrotta or Rote. As has been already remarked, it was the favourite accompaniment for the voice owing to its sweet tone.(1)

The double-pipe (ŠEM, Akkad. *ḥalḥallatu*) was frequently to be found in the hands of the *naru* musicians, sometimes combined with the timbrel or tambourine (ME-ZE): its strident tone, compared to the voice of the Wind God, was probably more serviceable in outdoor processions than the softer strains of the flute.

The appearance of the horn (SÎM) in the temple music is particularly interesting, and the fact that the ideogram for the "call horn" assumes a reduplicated form shows that the calls were composed of quickly reiterated notes or signals like those employed on the *Shophar* and *Khatsotserah*, the sacred horn and trumpet of the Hebrews. "Blow up the Shophar in the new moon" cries the psalmist (lxxxi. 3): may not this custom have been handed down from the Babylonian celebrations, when the crescent moon first appeared and on the great festival of the New Year's Day? In the Jewish ritual the trumpet was to be blown by the priests "in the beginning of your months over your burnt-offerings and the sacrifices of your peace-offerings: and ye shall be remembered before your God". In the same way the horn-blowing, while "the water was sprinkled and divine petitions offered", in the forecourt of the temple at Lagash "filling it with joy", and the similar sounds, which like "the voice of a bull" resounded within the walls of E-sira at Eridu, not only proclaimed a time of general rejoicing, but probably, like the sacred drum, was supposed to summon the deity to attention, a custom still lingering in Japan. How much was required in this way is shown by the frantic efforts of the Baal priests on Mount Carmel. At the door of each Buddhist temple a bell is to be seen still, which the believers strike "to attract the notice of the sleeping gods".

Of the drum almost enough has been said already. In earliest times there was no doubt the belief that the god—a royal personage slain for the welfare of his land and people—actually resided within it and spoke in its sounds: the placing of images of the gods within the body of the bronze kettledrum (LILIS), as described in an additional note to this chapter, shows how long this belief lingered: its connection with the ritual drum (BALAG) was explained in our opening chapter. The large LILIS was kept for use within the temple precincts, but a smaller and more portable form seems to have found a place in processions and, with the tambourines or timbrels—the rectangular A-DÂP and the round ME-ZE (manzu)—to have contributed its rhythmic beats to the fervour of the moment.

Of the sistrum, as has already been noted, we can discover no mention in the liturgies or in the regulations for acts of worship, although we certainly find it depicted in this connection on seals (Pl. II, 3, 5) and on the inlay of the royal harp found at Ur (Pl. VIII, 2), where a form of magic ritual is being parodied by animals or probably performed by men so disguised: we can only suggest that possibly at a comparatively early date it was superseded by some primitive kind of cymbals (katral). At any rate in the later periods many of the older instruments were not so much in evidence, though a Babylonian clay plaque (Pl. III, 2) shows the "divine lilissu" and the cymbals used by a man and woman to animate their companions in a boxing match, which was part of the ritual of magic known as devil-driving—the "fighting twins" being a charm against evil. To the war-loving Assyrians all things had to bow and serve their frenzied militarism, but the harp of Enlil and the temple flute were spared: probably they were not strong enough for outstanding display and the upright harp (zakkal) and the double-reed pipe were more effective.(2)

Having thus described in brief the use made of the musical instruments in the ordered worship of the Sumerians, we may here interpolate further remarks on the animal orchestras and the zoomorphic forms which so frequently appear in connection with the instruments themselves. The idea that the lower creation is conscious of the charm of musical sounds is age-long. Orpheus, in one guise or another, has from earliest days played his part in taming the fiercer passions of beast and bird. In the illustrations given on Plates IV, 1; VIII, 6, the shepherd with flute or with lute wins the appreciation of his dog and his flock: and the herdsmen, genii loci, with their sevenfold strains (Pl. VIII, 7) lead in ordered procession lion, antelope, sheep, ox, horse, panther and ostrich. As Friar Bartholomaeus Anglicus has noted in his De Proprietatibus Rerum of the thirteenth century of our era (to quote Trevisa's quaint translation of a century or so later): "Musyk abatyth maystry of evyl spryrytes in mankynde...and Musyk excyteth and comfortyth bestis and serpentes, foules and delphines to take hede therto."

But there is a further step in this association between man and the animal world, of which he is himself a member. From the early dynastic times of far-off Sumer to the days of mediaeval and modern art we find the animals themselves credited with the skill of the musician and offering the pleasures of the dance to their own kith and kin. In the person of the animal-musician on the seal from Ur (Pl. II, 2) as well as also on the limestone slabs from Tell Halaf (Pl. VIII, 1), wolf, lion, dog, cat, bear, monkey and other creatures are showing off their prowess as practical instrumentalists on lyre, cymbals, timbrel, pipe and "all kinds of music", while ox and ass tread the mazy dance; or as on Pl. V, 5.

What was the origin of this fantastic notion and how far was it seriously considered? Perhaps we may indicate its possible source and subsequent development in the following way.

In remote prehistoric ages man found himself in close contact with the world of nature: around him were creatures with gifts of sagacity and craftiness more capable and with strength and swiftness superior to his own. Partly from his inward consciousness and partly from superstitious reverence he attributed to them other qualities of which he was himself possessed. No doubt he had already observed the way in which many of them responded to his shrill whistle and call-horn; and the well-worn policy of attributing the highest place of honour to beings and creatures of questionable friendliness—which culminates in so-called devil-worship—bade him link them with himself in the highest enjoyment of music. In this first stage then the animal orchestra was a superstitious "mascot", a means of allaying suspicion and dread.

To this succeeded a second stage in which the animal orchestra was united to the ritual of worship by representative means, i.e. by masked men figuring as animals or birds. Mr Gadd points this out in connection with the Ur plaque (Pl. VIII, 2) and Dr Murray, in her book *The God of the Witches*, stresses this idea and would see in all representations of such mystic rites mummers and masqueraders. We do not consider this possible in every case; for, although human hands may be substituted for claws or hoofs in performance, the general form of the animal is undisguised. As a natural outcome, however, of human thought and expression it has maintained its hold on the worship of Asiatic, African and American primitives to our own day, and elaborate and awe-inspiring masks of beasts and birds play a considerable part in their ceremonial rites. In our own country within living memory the Dorset "oozer" or "ox-masked man" took part in certain moral performances, which were certainly allied to ancient animalism. As an instance of this stage a man, evidently wearing a bird mask, will be noticed on Plate V, 4: he holds in his hands the bow-shaped harp and is accompanying a singer. The slab, from which it is taken, dates from about the year 3000 B.C. and is said to represent some symbolic use, probably at a New Year's Festival of the Mother Goddess and the revival of Nature.

On an early dynastic slate tablet, discovered at Hierakonpolis in Upper Egypt, a man attired in a fox-mask is attracting with his pipe a wild bull, a goat and a giraffe either for the dance or for capture. On a frieze of the time of Ashurnasirpal (*c.* 870 B.C.) two mummers in lion skins and masks are performing on the lute. At Ras Shamra in North Syria a fourteenth-century seal shows priests evidently wearing animal or spirit masks.

The next step we may term the satirical outlook. It is here quite evident that neither superstition nor mystery found any part in the representation: it was evidently meant as parody such as we notice in the caricature of an Egyptian quartet of the reign of Rameses III (*c.* 1200 B.C.) depicted on the Turin Papyrus; there an ass on the harp, a lion on the lyre, a crocodile on the lute and a monkey on the double-pipe are making gallant music. The ass on the lyre became, in fact, a well-known proverb. Boethius has preserved and notes it and Chaucer in *Troilus and Creseide* uses it thus:

> What! Slombrest thow as in a lytargye?
> Or art thow lyk an asse to the harpe,
> That hereth soun, whan men the strenges plye,
> But in his minde of that no melodye
> May sinken, him to glade, for that he
> So dul is of his bestialitee?

In this category we may place such ludicrous carvings, found in mediaeval architecture, as the cat and fiddle, pig and bagpipe, fox and horn with other pointed allusions to minstrelsy.

Out of these covert thrusts at incapacity, however, there arose the higher idea which is associated with pious builders and sculptors of the Middle Ages, when on capital, corbel and gargoyle they portrayed in our cathedrals and churches the scenes of bygone days. "Let every thing that hath breath praise the Lord" sang the psalmist; and, if angels and men tuned their harps and viols in high accord, why should not the humbler creation join in the uplifted lay? So we find such a combination as that which adorns the fourteenth-century chapel and aisle of Cogges Church, Oxfordshire, where a man with a double-pipe and bells, a bear with the psaltery, a monkey with the harp, a dog with the gittern, a horse with pipe and tabor, a goat with the viol, a calf with the bagpipe and a cowherd with his horn swell the grand acclaim.

It is then in the worship of praise—the praise of all creation—we have still perpetuated the animal orchestra of primitive man.

The animal form, however, was not confined to the musicians: it was even developed on the instrument itself. Instances abound in our own day. The peacock-lute (*Tayus*) of India is strikingly modelled after the form of the beautiful bird. In Burmah and Siam we find crocodile-zithers (*Meyoung*); in China and Japan tiger-shaped harmonicas. Birds' heads are of course common on stringed instruments; the dragon's head on horns. In Africa there are tortoise-shaped drums and in Central and South America the figures of men, reptiles and birds are moulded into whistles and flageolets. The Chinese ritual flute (*Ti*) has a dragon's head and tail; while many of our own instruments imitate in shape and decoration the features of man and beast.

It was so too in the dynastic—even predynastic—Sumerian days. The lyre, found in its simplest form in Subaraic and Semitic cultures, was adorned with a bull's or heifer's head, as seen in the lyres of Fara and Ur. At Lagash towards the close of the third millennium the complete figure of the animal stands on the sound-board (Pl. VIII, 3), as does that of a stag on the boat-shaped lyre of earlier date from Ur (Pl. VII, 2). But in some cases the whole body of the instrument is transformed into the animal form, with head, body (sound-chest) and legs (Pl II, 1, 5), though the short legs also appear on the lyre without the bull's head, as on the Larsa potsherd.

It is difficult to give a definite reason for the favour shown in this respect to the bull: its frequency at Ur suggests some connection with Nannar, the horned Moon-God and patron of the city; but it is also found at Fara and Lagash and the stag is a variant decoration. Amongst the pre-historic Subaraean population Teshub, the Great God, was worshipped under the form of a bull and appears to have been in this respect identical with the Semitic Ishkur or Adad, the Wind God, "exalted bull, son of Enlil". Can it be that in this way was commemorated the reputed origin of the lyre, when, from its strings, "that grand old Harper", as he is called, "the God of Winds, drew sounds of deep delight"? For the going forth of Ishkur, though terrible in the great storm, could be "as a low-voiced breeze, a breeze of gentle sound". It will be remembered that in the Psalm of Meditation on the Harp (AL) the vibrations of the deep strings, rising over the walls of the temple court, are described as like "the voice of a horned bull", so it may have been thought appropriate to the deep sounds. At any rate we know that both bull and stag were cult-animals, which may account for their decorative use in this and other ways.

On the horizontal Assyrian harp (*Eširtu*) shown on Plate XII, 9 it will be noticed that a small open hand terminates the upright bar. It cannot be a music-holder, as has been suggested from modern analogy, but it may be of the "mascot" type; for at the head of a long-necked rustic lute used in India as early as the Sanskrit Period, though now played with a bow and still in use in Southern India and Turkestan, there is placed the representation of an open hand. The instrument is called *Rāvanahasta*—or the Hand of Rāvana, the God of Fate, an evilly-disposed deity, who needs propitiation.

From the paintings on the walls of Egyptian temples and tombs we gather that this form of decoration was frequently used on their instruments; on the harps appear the head of Horus, God of Light, Joy and Victory, or (as at Dendera) that of Khum, Lord of Creation. On the sistrum Hathor, the Goddess-Mother and Mistress of the Dance, is depicted, while Plutarch observed that, just below the fork, were to be seen the faces of Isis on one side, and of Nephtys on the other (i.e. resurrection and death); on the top the figure of a cat with human face signified the manifold life-giving powers of the good goddess. So too our mediaeval craftsmen adorned their instruments "with visage grim and fair".(3)

In conclusion we will give some idea of the ways in which music was performed; for, through the research of Assyriologists, we are able to analyse the various types of psalms, liturgies and hymns, which so constantly supply the subject of the tablet records.

The earliest order for public worship was naturally of a simple kind, consisting of libations and a supplication, in hymn form, accompanied by the flute, the double-pipe or the lyre. Sometimes only the sacred drum was employed, a use still prevalent in India. In a Lamentation over Nippur the psalmist is directed to "sing to the drum (BALAG)": and even the other drums, set probably in the temple court, were admitted at times to provide a rhythmic background. "To the little drum (UB) and to the large drum (A-LA) I sing" says a worshipper. This use of the two drums is not peculiar to Mesopotamia: in the Chinese Confucian temple a small instrument is hung beside the large drum in the courtyard and after each line of the Hymn to the Master there is a stroke on the large instrument and a tap on the small drum or pair of small drums attached to it. Before the next line is sung the bell is struck.

At a later date the services were prolonged into a set liturgy, composed of four or more hymns and (for the period) elaborate choral and instrumental renderings, if we may trust the orchestral cues. Certain portions too of the liturgy appear to have been taken in recitative. The following directions given for the order of ritual at the dedication of the foundation of a temple will illustrate this arrangement.

The appointed priests, first of all, performed the magical rites necessary for purification and consecration: the psalmists were required to attend to chant the opening petition and the proper psalms: a professional musician (NAR) had to accompany them. The chief psalmist was then directed to sing a hymn to the Gods Ea, Shamash and Marduk, with a double-pipe accompaniment; and the service closed with the stirring strains of an epic poem. Dr Langdon remarks that this final chorus was no part of the more ancient Sumerian use, and suggests that it may have been sung congregationally by all present, as a well-known hymn. Except on such an occasion as this, the *asipu* or priest of magic generally took no part in the ceremonial worship of the temple.(4)

Very little is told us in the early records of what we may call "private" temple prayer, though the forecourt must have been open for such a purpose.

It appears to have been termed šu-ILLA or "the lifting of the hand" and a trained musician might accompany it. In a Hymn to Ishtar of the Isin Period (*c.* 2100 B.C.) the suppliant says "with the strains of the lyre (AL-GAR), whose sound is sweet, I will speak to thee": and, in the lament of a penitent, his crying is likened to the plaintive sound of the reed-pipe, NÂ, which was probably linked with his petition.

Dr Ebeling has published a very instructive list of Sumerian and Assyrian songs, which show a large range of compositions. Apparently it is a catalogue of some musical library made in the ninth or eighth century B.C., and Dr Langdon and Dr Ebeling himself have furnished translations. It affords, even though imperfect, a remarkable insight into the wealth of musical material available at this and a yet earlier date. It embraces a wide field of subjects, comprising liturgies, royal psalms, festal songs and hymns of lamentation: there are poems of victory and heroism, folk-songs for craftsmen and shepherds, musical recitations and a long list of love-songs for both sexes. It is tantalising that only the first lines of the poems are given and that only about half of the tablet, which was in eight columns, has been preserved. But we are able to gather from the details available and so far as instrumental references are extant that, while the temple liturgies in Sumerian demanded the accompaniment of the flute (TI-GI) or the square timbrel (A-DÂP), the recitations in Akkadian and the love-ditties rejoiced in the ten-stringed harp (*eširtu*), the Syrian reed-pipe (*imbubu* or *malilu*), the "curved" pipe (*pîtu*) and the "covered" pipe (*kitmu*); the last-named being especially favoured by women, like the bulbed reed-pipes of the Etruscans and the Egyptians of the New Empire.(5)

It is difficult to appraise the effect of all this Sumerian music and song, because both in scale and composition it differs radically from our modern ideas. Their music must have been evolved without regard to modal characteristics, and although we may now fit the scale they employed into the ecclesiastical Lydian Mode or the ancient Hypolydian Mode with its mingled religious fervour and sensuous tenderness, any such ascription to the music, in the Greek sense of the term "mode", would certainly be an anachronism for so remote a date as the early centuries of the second millennium B.C. In the lines of their poems, if we may so describe them, there appears to be no kind of metre or fixed number of syllables, though there are frequent traces of an inclination to divide the line into two halves by a slight pause. Like the earliest Byzantine hymns, the composition is a form of rhythmical prose.

From the only example of musical accompaniment at present discovered (although it is known that the Sumerian Hymn on Creation is but a section of a longer and continuous poem) it is evident that most of the words were sung in free recitative (*recitativo secco*), the verbal accentuation giving the rhythm, which was reinforced by the harp or the drum accompaniment. To have rendered this successfully and artistically must have required much study and practice, undertaken no doubt in the choir-schools attached to the temples, where the traditional method would be orally handed down and carefully preserved. The importance attached to a correct rendering may be inferred from the attempt made, in connection with this particular hymn, to fix the tradition by some form of notation. In Greek music the accents, used by the grammarians to mark the inflections of the speaking voice, were ultimately employed for a like purpose—to remind singers of what they had learned by ear—becoming when developed the mediaeval Neumatic Notation. Before dealing, however, with the disputed question of melodic intonation we may draw attention to some of the methods employed in rendering these ancient poetical compositions, not necessarily with instrumental accompaniment.

A very early instance of antiphonal use is given by Mr Sidney Smith in *Notes on the Gutian Period* (J.R.A.S. 1932). It is a Lament, preserved on a tablet written at Babylon in 297 B.C., but consisting of a much older text dating from the last quarter of the third millennium B.C. In it women of various Sumerian and Akkadian towns are called upon to mourn their fate under the Gutian oppressors. The towns mentioned fall into two geographical groups centering around Erech (Sumerian) and Agade (Akkadian) and they appear to be represented by two semi-choruses, each singing alternate lines appropriate to their respective groups. If so, it is a forerunner of "programme" music.

A more elaborate scheme is set out in a Liturgy and Prayer to the Moon God, written a little later during the IIIrd Dynasty of Ur and described by Dr Langdon in his *Babylonian Liturgies*. The first six lines form an introduction in which a single chanter appeals to the god Sin, as watchman of the Temple of Enlil and patron of the flocks and the harvest. Then follow ten strophes of four lines each after the manner of a litany; lines one and three of each section have a recurring refrain beginning "O Nannar, God of Wisdom art thou" or "God of Light are thou", whilst the intermediate lines tell of some aspect of the god in respect of the fields. This section would evidently have been rendered by chanter and chorus or by two semi-choruses antiphonally. Then there is a short recitative by the chanter describing Enlil's orders to Sin with an appeal for his return to Ur; and the whole concludes with a chorus rejoicing in the anticipated fulfilment of Enlil's commands. We have already given some idea of the musical accompaniment (if any) for so highly finished a composition as this in our description of the foundation ritual for a new temple.

It is conceivable that compositions in recitative form were preferably allotted, as in the earliest Byzantine use, to a solo singer because he could permit himself much more freedom of time and accent than would have been possible in a choral rendering. In our transcription of the Creation Hymn, however, the whole has been given in fixed time by the use of crotchets. This crude method has been adopted to indicate roughly the probable accentual stresses placed on the original words, which we have also endeavoured to imitate in the English version. Like the *neumes* of the old Plainsong, it is not "measured" music.

A closer analysis of this accompanied Hymn appears to show that it falls into five sections or episodes. The opening section A (lines 1–11) may have been rendered by one chanter and section B (lines 12–20) taken by another, who was answered by yet a third solo singer in section C (lines 21–26). In the following section D (lines 27–58), which constitutes the main body of the composition, there seems to be a decided change in the style of the music: there is less recitative and more inclination to place note against syllable: this section may have been treated as a choral interlude, the subject-matter reminding us somewhat of a table of commandments to be kept by all. The appeal to Aruru, the great Goddess-Mother, which opens section E, would again be rendered by a solo chanter, who closed the song with the recitative lines of the final verses. As has already been stated, the full score of the hymn will be found after the Notes on the Chapters.

Since Dr Landsberger has affirmed that the syllabic signs, attached to this hymn, have no connection with music, it may add to our appreciation of the present attempt to interpret them musically, if we can find in that interpretation traces of expression illustrative of the words. An examination of the instrumental part in comparison with the original words will show that such expression is not lacking. We may, for instance, mention the solemn beat of the low notes in lines 2, 7–11, 18, 51, 67–9, where the gods and their worship are the prominent thoughts; or the "questioning" phrases in lines 16 and 17, 19 and 20, where the music rises or falls sympathetically; or the "busy" feeling of the main section, which so well portrays man's ceaseless toil, relieved by feast and holy day. If, moreover, we accept the suggestion that the last two lines (70–1) were added for use in some particular temple, the actual close of the hymn on the simple diatonic passage (C, D, E), slowly rendered, must have been intensely stately and impressive. The soloists would probably have ornamented their chant with those grace-notes so beloved by Orientals.

Since our elucidation of the Sumerian notation signs, the opportunity has occurred of consulting an instructive paper by Dr E. Sievers, entitled *Beiträge zur babylonischen Metrik* (Z.A. xxxviii). In it the writer applies himself to the difficult task of *Schall-analyse*, that is, of recovering from the accentual stress on the Sumerian or Akkadian words the melodic intonation of the chant or hymn. Taking as his subject two well-known groups of poems—the Ishtar Hymns (as transcribed by M. Thureau-Dangin) and the Fourth Table of the World-Creation

Epic (Wehtsch and Zimmern), he notes, first of all, that they both belong to the class of compositions known as strophic, the lines themselves being either contrasted with one another or more frequently falling, as hemistiches, into half-line sections. We have already mentioned the fact that the Greek musicians of a later day made use of the well-known accents to express a vocal notation; and this writer has also so employed them, though of course they form no part of the original texts. A single rising sound (*Steigton*) is denoted by the acute accent (′) and a single descending sound (*Fallton*) by the grave accent (`). The circumflex (^) he also uses to express a "divided" sound-sequence, that is, a drop from a high to a low note like the neumatic *clivis*: and he takes the inverted circumflex (ˇ) to denote, as the neumatic *podatus*, a lower sound followed by a higher. These two sequences he considers are the marks of the older music. In addition to these he has two "doubled" accents to express either the interval of a rising third (″) or that of a falling third (‶), which he says was a studied interval and not a mere aberration. So such diagrammatic representations of intonation as these appear: ∴ or .·′ or ·., etc.

The drawback to this old system of notation is that inherent in all such neumatic devices, namely, that it is difficult to know how high or how low the sounds, represented by them, are apart, though some help is here afforded by the "doubled" accents. We may, therefore, well ask whether the circumflex accents denote the intervals of a fourth, or a fifth or more; and also are they "slides" from one note to another or "leaps"? Mr Fox Strangways (*Music of Hindostan*) considers that in the very ancient *Saman* chant of India, as in the modern *Raga*, the intervals were taken as "leaps" in ascent and as "slides" in descent. It may have been so in Babylonia, considering their known connection. The men of old knew how to read them, however, because they had already learnt the intonations by oral instruction. They were content to do so. But it was not until the stave—first one line, then two, then more—gave a clue to their tonal positions that the problem was solved by an eye-picture.

It is easily recognized that in ordinary speech and more particularly in rhetorical utterance the voice rises and falls; but the question is whether such inflections in these early times were based on some acknowledged system? Dr Sievers appears to consider that they were, and that they formed a chant or song (*Melodieführung*) of definite intervals.

With this view we are on the whole in accord, though whether his signs are rightly applied to the words over which they stand is a matter for the poet, linguist and elocutionist to decide. At any rate the voice-part elicited from the "magadised" harp-notation of the Creation Hymn shows that these same intervals were in actual use, although this poem is not distinctly of the strophic class. As an example of their use the opening lines of the hymn will be quite sufficient; for, placing the above-mentioned intonation signs over the musical score, we have the following *Schall-analyse*:

Intonation Signs
Line 1 ∧   2 \   3 // /   4 /   5 //   //   6 / /   7 ∧   8 \   12 ∨

4th   Low   Ascending   High   3rd   Tones   5th de-   3rd de-   4th
descending   note   tones   note   ascending ascending scending scending ascending

And so throughout the hymn, though the pitch of the singer's voice, around which the inflections weave themselves, may change from time to time. This is a detail which neither accents nor neumatic signs in their simple and early forms are able to express. Such a coincidence may suggest that our reading of the musical notation signs is probably on the right lines.

In conclusion, and after a careful survey of a large number of these ritual compositions of various periods, we should probably be correct in assuming that the Classical Age of Sumerian Art fell within the second half of the third miliennium B.C. and the first half of the second millennium. With the advent of the Kassite Dynasty it apparently lost its encouragement and in the Renaissance, which arose under the Assyrian and Babylonian Empires of the first half of the first millennium, the practice of compiling song-services out of old refrains and overloading them with a wearisome repetition of names and titles, divine and royal, shows a distinct decadence in poetic originality. True artistic appreciation had faded out.

ADDITIONAL NOTE I

THE RITUAL FOR THE HEADING OF THE KETTLEDRUM

The following instructions for furnishing with a skin-head the bronze LILIS (*Lilissu*) or kettledrum are taken from tablets found at Warka (Erech) of the Seleucid Period (*c.* 300 B.C.) and now in the Museum at Brussels, together with a tablet (O 175) containing a summary of priestly theology on one side, and on the other line drawings of the drum and the bull which provided the necessary skin (Pl. III, 4). The translation in full with notes will be found in *Rituels Accadiens* (1921) by Thureau-Dangin, and in the *Revue d'Assyriologie*, vol. XVI, pp. 145 f. (with illustration) by the same author.

A summary of the principal tablet (AO 6479), which, according to a final note, was "written and revised according to the ancient original", is as follows: A bull without defect, black in colour and untouched by stick or whip was selected; if spotted with seven groups of white spots in star-form, it was unsuitable. The animal was brought to the "House of Knowledge" (the temple) on a propitious day and offerings were made to the great Gods and especially to Lumḫa (Ea), God of Music and Wisdom. A reed mat was placed on the ground and covered with sand: on it the animal was held. More offerings were made and perfumes burnt. A torch was then lighted and the bull was singed. Twelve linen cloths were laid on the ground and twelve bronze images of the

Gods of Heaven, Earth and the Underworld placed upon them. Sacrifices were made and the body or bowl of the drum was set in its place. The animal's mouth was washed and, by means of a tube of aromatic reed, incantations were whispered into its ears explaining, in dialectical Sumerian, the honour which was about to be done to the bull by its divine use. A hymn was next chanted to the accompaniment of the double reed-pipe. The bull was then slain, its heart burnt, and the body, after it had been skinned, wrapped in a red cloth. The skin was treated with fine flour, beer, wine, grease, Hittite alum and gall-nut. It was then stretched over the bowl of the drum and tied round with a cord. Pins or pegs of box, cedar, ebony and other woods were driven through the skin into holes previously made in the body of the drum and, to render all taut, the tendon of the bull's left shoulder was twisted round the edge of the drum-head, the twelve bronze images of the gods having been previously placed inside the bowl. The first cord was then undone and, at a later time, an ornamental binding was placed over the edges of the skin, the pin-heads being also wrapped round with coloured wools and varnished. The now deified bull was bidden to guard well the sacred images within. On the fifteenth day after, sacrifices were again offered and the drum was carried into the presence of the temple gods. Only the initiated were allowed to witness these rites, and the drum became "The Divine *Lilissu*".

ADDITIONAL NOTE 2

"NEBUCHADREZZAR'S ORCHESTRA"

In preparing this little treatise we have frequently been asked what was the true composition of the orchestra mentioned by the English translators of our Authorised Version of the Bible in the third chapter of the Book of Daniel. As this is probably the sole specimen of Babylonian or Chaldean music popularly known, a few words on the subject may not be out of place.

In the revised edition of Sir John Stainer's *Music of the Bible* (1914) we dealt with many of the more doubtful points, and some of these have since been elucidated by recent discoveries.

To begin, however, with the original text. There is strong reason for believing that portions of the Book of Daniel were written at a much later date than the days of Nebuchadrezzar—to use the more correct form of the name—King of Babylon from 604 till 561 B.C. A considerable number of later Persian words (such as "satraps", A.V. "governors") appear, and many of the names of the musical instruments mentioned are adapted from Greek titles. It is therefore most probable that parts of the book were either compiled or considerably revised in the days of Greek culture and after the Persian influence, that is, during such a period as the reign of Antiochus Epiphanes (175–164 B.C.), when the Persian monarchy had fallen before the conquests of Alexander the Great: there are other reasons too for placing the probable date during the time of this Syrian Dynasty.

The musical instruments, of which the names are given in the Aramaic, which supplanted Hebrew, are as follows: *kar*e*na, mash*e*rokitha, kath*e*ros, sab*e*ka, p*e*santerin, sumponyah*, the superscript "e" denoting a very slight vowel sound. The Septuagint (Greek) version gives *salpinx, syrinx, kithara, sambuke, psalterion, sumphonia*: and the Vulgate *tuba, fistula, cithara, sambuca, psalterium, symphonia*. Josephus in his *Antiquities of the Jews* (x. 10) shortens the list by mentioning only the trumpet (*salpinx*).

In our principal English Versions we have:

Wicklif and Hereford: trumpe, pipe, harpe, sambuke, sawtrie, symphony;
Genevan Version: cornet, trumpet, harpe, sackebut, psalterie, dulcimer;
Authorised Version: cornet, flute, harp, sackbut, psaltery, dulcimer (Chald. symphony);
Revised Version: cornet, flute, harp, sackbut, psaltery, dulcimer (or bagpipe).

The word translated "cornet" is the horn or trumpet, for in early times no particular distinction was drawn between the two instruments: it is the Syrian *kar*ᵉ*na* and may be equated with the KARAN (*karana, kurna*) described in Chapter II (*c*). The Old English "cornet" was an instrument of wood and leather pierced with finger-holes and fitted with a trumpet-like mouthpiece. It was very popular when the Genevan and Authorised Versions were made. The "flute" was no doubt of the vertical type, the Hebrew *ugab* explained in Chapter II (*a*). In Syriac *mashrukitho* is the *zaffârah*, the Arab and Persian *sâfûre*, now a whistle-headed flute. The name is connected with the Hebrew root *sharak* "to hiss or whistle", derived from the sound made, like the Greek *syrinx* which, from its earlier form as a simple reed (*Syrinx monocalamos*), became the pan-pipes (*Syrinx polucalamos*). The "harp" is the large lyre of the Greeks (*kitharis*), the *cithara* of Roman days. The "sackbut" represents the *sambuca* or *sab*ᵉ*ka*, a smaller seven-stringed lyre (Ch. III (*b*)); we may render it by the Old English word "rote". This translation of the later English versions "sackbut" (an instrument now called the trombone) was probably derived from Wicklif's *sambuke*— a nasalized form of the Syrian *sab*ᵉ*ka*: it became in Latin *sambuca* and was confused with *sambucus*, a pipe made of elder wood. The sackbut appeared in England at the beginning of the sixteenth century. In English mediaeval literature the *sambuca* is a reed-blown pipe like the shawm or oboe, though the Boulogne Psalter (ninth century) correctly gives, as an illustration of the *sambuca*, an instrument of the lyre type. The "psaltery" or *Psalterion*— the change to *Psanterin* is on philological lines—was a box-like instrument with strings plucked by the fingers (Ch. III (*d*)). It is the parent of the *Santîr* and *Pi-santîr* ("little psaltery"), commonly struck now in Persia with two small sticks like a dulcimer.

The "dulcimer" of the English translation is supposed to represent the *sumponyah* of the Aramaic, a name evidently derived from the Greek *sumphonia*, becoming in Latin *symphonia* and in Early English "*symphonye*". The original meaning of the word was simply "a concord of sounds"; but during our present era it has been applied to numerous instruments capable of producing some sort of harmony. About 400 A.D. Prudentius gives this name to the double-reed pipe as a signal for battle amongst the Egyptians. Venantius Fortunatus in the next century considered it a pipe *plena suo flatu* "big with its own wind"—probably a bagpipe. Isidore in the seventh century applies it to a double-headed drum: still later the clavichord, a keyboard relative of the dulcimer, was so called, and in mediaeval times, under the form *chifonie*, it became a common name for the hurdy-gurdy: even now as the *zampogna* it is said to supply a popular title for the Calabrian bagpipe and the Dalmatian double flageolet, though some would derive this word from *sambucna*, a contracted form of *sambucina* "a little pipe". The Jewish commentators of the Middle Ages generally treat the *sumphonia* as a double-pipe or a bagpipe.

It will, however, be noticed that the indisputable use of this word (and its derivatives) as the name of a musical instrument is confined to our own era, and the point to be decided is, For what did the word stand in pre-Christian centuries? Aristotle and Plato in their writings of the fourth century B.C. use it in its original sense as a "harmony of sounds", or more properly of two sounds, i.e. fourth, fifth or octave. With them it is no musical instrument, though a form of bagpipe was already known; their predecessor, Aristophanes, in his *Lysistrata* speaks of the *physeteria* and the *physallides*—"bellow" and "bladder pipes"—as accompanying a dance, the use of the plural forms of the words corresponding to our "bagpipes" and showing that two sounding-tubes at least were employed. A possibly early kind of bagpipe from Susa is shown on Plate IV, 5.

In Polybius' account of the mad freaks of Antiochus Epiphanes the word *sumphonia* is used (if we take it in its natural sense) of "a union of many instruments in accord", in modern phraseology "a band of musicians". The king summons his band to attend and then dances to their music: or, on other occasions, he suddenly appears at a banquet playing on a horn-pipe (*keration*), or, as some would suggest, carrying a wine jar (*keramion*), attended again by his musicians. It is important to mark the use of the word in this sense at this particular time, because it is contemporary with the presumed date of this portion of the Book of Daniel, as noted above. In the first century of our era *symphonia* constantly appears in the works of Horace, Cicero, Seneca, Pliny and others, but always as "a concord of sounds" or "a company of musicians": for Horace "a band" out-of-tune mars the feast: for Cicero at a grand banquet "a band" plays and *symphoniae* are "musical parties": Seneca tells us of "singing to the accompaniment of a band" (*symphonia*).

The natural interpretation of all these and other allusions rules out the idea of "the bagpipe", which, we must remember, had in this same century its own particular names and was giving them to the players, as Martial's *ascaules* and Suetonius' *utricularius*. Dion Chrysostom, the orator, in a speech delivered in the days of Nero or shortly after, alludes to the skilful man who "could pipe with his mouth and the bag under his armpits"— evidently a bagpiper, but with no mention of the name *symphonia* as given to the instrument.

It is interesting too to notice the use of the word by St Luke in his record of the Parable of the Prodigal Son (xv. 25). Probably the original was spoken in Aramaic and the ordinary word *zamar* ("singing" or "music") would have been used: it is still the translation of the Syriac version. Moreover St Jerome in his commentary on this passage says that "the *symphonia* is not a kind of instrument, as some Latin writers think, but it is 'concordant harmony'. It is expressed in Latin by *consonantia*". *Consonare*, we know, was used in the Augustan Age not only for choral music but for a concert of pipes and other instruments. This remark of St Jerome clearly shows that in 407 A.D. he, who knew the languages and customs of the East so well by long continued residence, was aware that the use of this word for the name of an instrument was comparatively recent, as our literary evidence also shows.

From the facts therefore here adduced it appears very doubtful whether the word used in the Book of Daniel refers to an instrument at all. Dr Pusey in his *Lectures on Daniel* (p. 29) seems to have come to the same conclusion, though reluctantly. It looks as if some revision of the text was responsible for its appearance for, whereas our English version omits the word in verse 7, the Aramaic gives it only in verses 5, 10 (mis-spelt) and 15. The older Septuagint version has it only in verse 15, while Theodotion's version supplies it in verses 5, 7 and 10: the Vulgate on the other hand uses it in each of the five passages. This suggests great variations in the original texts consulted. It certainly has not received the care and attention bestowed upon the names of the other instruments nor, if it is a wind instrument, does it take its place with the rest of its kind. It would, we consider, be quite possible to give to it its legitimate interpretation as the combined effect of various instruments. The passage appears to require some such word because the signal to the vast concourse was intended to be given by a grand outburst, the *tutti*, of the great orchestra. We would therefore translate the passage thus: "at what time ye hear the sound of the trumpet, flute, lyre, rote, psaltery and the full consort, even of all kinds of music". This last item would include the many percussion instruments, drums, cymbals, etc. so prominent in Oriental performances; and the phrase "full consort" is used in the sixteenth and seventeenth centuries for "many instruments played together". The final "and" of the text means "that is, even, namely, or to wit" and follows the frequent use of the Hebrew copulative *waw explicativum* (Gesenius, *Heb. Gram.* in Cowley Ed., p. 484), as it does also of the Greek particle (*kai*). If the word *sumphonia* does not here refer to an instrument and is partially explained by the words which follow it, its existence in the texts would naturally be precarious, as seemingly redundant in the opinion of the scribes.

In conclusion we may say that the list of instruments given for this orchestra shows a marked departure from the recognized formation displayed in the times of the Assyrian and Second Babylonian Empires. Its composition is much more Graeco-Syrian. Had it been really organized in the days of Nebuchadrezzar, the large upright harp (*zakkal*) and the ten-stringed harp (*eširtu*) would certainly have appeared, while the place of the flute (*syrinx*) would have been taken by the well-known reed-pipes (*ḫalḫallatu*) or more probably by the later double-reed pipes (*imbube*).

CHAPTER VI

The Racial Element in Music

THE probability of any connection between music and racial affinity may at first sight appear to be but slight; but it is a subject which is now receiving marked attention, stimulated by the ethnographical researches of the late Dr E. von Hornbostel, Dr Curt Sachs and others, especially with reference to the scales and instruments still in use among peoples of primitive culture. Moreover, a perusal of the preceding pages must have convinced the reader that in the use and development of several of the Sumerian musical instruments there are many evident indications of a common relationship with other cultural centres, either through ancestral descent or by commercial association. It is so in our own country; the old English harp with its bent fore-pillar links us in kinship with Scandinavia and the Norsemen, while the long-necked lute displays a later trade connection with Southern Europe.

Taking then two or three types most characteristic of the earlier inhabitants of the Mesopotamian plain, such facts as these present themselves. The use of the lyre, which is very general, is a connecting link with districts westward of that country rather than with those on the east, where the lyre type is unknown. On the other hand the bow-shaped harp claims a close affinity with similar instruments found to the east and north-east of the Land of Sumer. Again, the peculiar hour-glass-shaped drum carries our thoughts eastward also even to distant China where it is acknowledged as an ancient gift from "the barbarians of the West". It was in the Indus valley early in the third millennium, B.C.

It may be objected, however, that some of these instruments presuppose a connection with the South and that both the lyre and bow-shaped harp are traceable in the ancient land of Egypt from the days of the Old Empire. That is true; but as the lyre in its most primitive form is distinctly a Semitic instrument and was so recognized by the Egyptians themselves, it probably reached them, as it did the Sumerians, through the Semitic tribes of Northern Arabia and the eastern shores of the Mediterranean Sea. As for the bow-shaped harp called *ban* or *ben* in Egypt, there is every reason to believe that it came, together with its name meaning "bow" and not an Egyptian word, from the Sumerians, of whose language the word formed a part.

It may have been brought through commercial interchange or perhaps through the extended influence of migration south-westward. This striking transplantation of a purely Asiatic instrument to the African continent and the general distribution and development of this harp are more fully explained in an additional note to this chapter.

With regard to the hour-glass-shaped drum, it is sufficient to say that it found no place in ancient Egypt at all, although it now occurs occasionally amongst certain East African tribes.(1)

Such facts as these may perhaps be thought insignificant and unimportant, but they have a direct bearing on cultural relationship and on the origin of the Sumerians, which at present is involved in so much obscurity. For instance, a view has been put forward with some insistence that they came from the regions of Abyssinia and Somaliland during the fourth millennium B.C., and gave their superior civilization to the benighted inhabitants of Southern Mesopotamia.

If this were so and they were intimately connected with pre-dynastic or early dynastic Egyptians—if not actually recalcitrant Egyptians themselves expelled from their country!—should we not have expected to find traces of these early Sumerian instruments in the records and representations of their supposed earlier home-land, especially in alliance with their religious worship? This, as has been stated, we fail to do.

Whence then came they and when?

The general opinion now held is that the Sumerians descended from the eastern or north-eastern side of Mesopotamia. We say descended, because they were evidently hill-folk worshipping their gods in high places, hence the lofty temple-towers or *ziggurats*, which they built when they found themselves in the rich and fertile plain of the Two Rivers. So the question which immediately presents itself is whether this favoured district, which had been formed and forming amid countless centuries through the alluvial deposits of the Euphrates and Tigris, had already been occupied by some other race of mankind. Dr Frankfort, in his exhaustive treatise on *Archaeology and the Sumerian Problem* (1932), comes to the conclusion that the Sumerians were not only the main authors of the civilization but were the earliest occupants of the southern land. If so, they were responsible for the First Cultural Period (Al-Ubaid). But many other authorities think that this cannot be accepted and is improbable. They consider that the new-comers arrived at the *end* of the First Period and thus gave the impetus to the remarkable culture of the Second Period (Uruk). So rapid an advance seems to demand the infiltration of a different race of men.

On this matter too little attention, we consider, has been given to the Hebrew traditions of the early homes of mankind as set out in the opening chapters of the Book of Genesis. There is no reason to suppose that they are less trustworthy than the somewhat similar traditions handed down by Babylonian scribes, especially when we remember that the racial affinities of the nations of the earth, both in their extent and in their limitations, were of the utmost importance to

PLATE X. PERCUSSION INSTRUMENTS

1. Sumerian Sign for BALAG (Drum)
2. Sumerian Signs for UB (Hand Drum)
3. Sumerian Sign for ḤUL, "to rejoice" (Harp?)
4. Chinese Sign for TIK, TEK or TI (Vertical Flute)
5. Chinese Sign for TSU-KU ("Footed" Drum)
6. Chinese Hour-glass-shaped Drum (*Čang Ku*)
7. Tibetan Skull Drum (*Čang Teu*)
8. Indian or Sivas Drum (*Damaru*)
9. Soudanese Drum
10. Syrian Drum (*Tabil šamî*)
11. Assyrian Long Drum—from a bas-relief
12. Telugu Drum (*Ghutru*)
13. Egyptian Drum (*Darabukke*)
14. Dervish Drum (*Baz*)
15. Persian Drum (*Donbek*)
16. African Drum, North Togoland
17. Assyrian Hand Drum—from a bas-relief
18. Moroccan Square Timbrel (*Deff*)
19. Muscovite Drum—after Praetorius, 1619
20. Arabian Round Timbrel (*Ghirbāl*)
21. "Spur-shaped" Sistrum, Egypt; *c.* 2160 B.C.
22. Georgian Sistrum, Transcaucasia
23. Abyssinian Sistrum (*Dsanâdsel*)
24. "Temple-shaped" Sistrum, Ancient Egypt
25. "Stirrup-shaped" Sistrum, Ancient Egypt
26. Assyrian Cymbals—from a bas-relief

PLATE X

the exclusive Hebrews. Their well-known story is that the Edin or Plain of "Shinar", which probably means "the Two Rivers", was inhabited by man long before the arrival of city-builders or representatives of the higher cultures implied by the use of metal and the development of art. This primitive settlement at the head of the Persian Gulf (as it was afterwards called) in which, according to Bible story and an old Sumerian poem, "men wore no garments and ate herbs" was scattered by a catastrophe. From the sacred writers' point of view it was owing to moral delinquency. But it was no doubt also due to some physical disturbance, of which we think a hint is given by "the flashing light, like that from a sword, turning every way". This suggests the emanation of those gaseous vapours which so frequently underlie maritime and alluvial deposits such as were present in "the Sea Land" on which they lived. At the beginning of our own era Pliny, in his *Natural History*, mentions the ebullition of naphtha at the head of the Gulf, for he says "at Susa it comes from fifteen apertures, the greatest of which also burns in the daytime; the Plain of Babylon too throws up a flame from a place like a fish-pond an acre in extent". Their early home was therefore deserted and although part of the population, represented by Seth, remained in the neighbourhood as a pastoral people and tillers of the soil, the rest, represented by Cain, passed into "the Land of Nod" eastward and became city-builders, artisans and cattle-breeders.

At the opening of the third century B.C. a Babylonian priest named Berosus wrote an account of his home-land. For the early period his information seems to have been derived from and built on religious traditions chiefly of a magical nature. His account is that weird creatures, half fish and half men, appeared out of the "Red Sea" (that is, the Persian Gulf) and that these were in some way connected with the Water-God, Ea of Eridu, the acknowledged patron of art and learning. But unfortunately Ea was not the god of the salt waters but of the "sweet waters"—a name applied to those subterranean springs which supplied the fresh and invigorating well-water.

The supposition therefore that the new civilization, with its increased knowledge, reached Southern Mesopotamia by way of the sea cannot be relied on. More probability rests with the Biblical tradition recorded in the eleventh chapter of Genesis, namely, that "they journeyed from the east, that they found a plain in the land of Shinar; and they dwelt there".

Who then were these new arrivals, who appear to have adopted many of the concepts of the early inhabitants, but impressed upon them the higher culture of a different race through peaceful penetration?

The answer it is difficult to give, because, with our present incomplete knowledge of the past, theories may be and have been broached only to be disproved by fresh discoveries. A short summary, however, of some of the suggestions offered may be useful to the general reader, and a fuller account of them can be obtained from the works of reference mentioned in the notes to this chapter.

We have already said that Dr Frankfort considers that the Sumerians were the original and first settlers in the land; that they came from the Iran highlands is his opinion. There is ample evidence that the people were a mixed race; this has been shown by the discovery of the remains of long-headed men and also of broad-headed men. Some writers consider that in the First Period no evidence of the presence of broad-headed men is forthcoming and that the inhabitants were not Sumerians but Arabs (that is, Semites) or perhaps Elamites or possibly a southward expansion of Subaraean or Hurrian types. Ethnologists have connected the incursive newcomers of the Second Period with the Dravidians of India, who are also found still in Baluchistan; it is acknowledged that among these tribes there has been at some unknown date an infiltration of a strongly broad-headed stock, known as Alpines, from the uplands of Central Asia. Philologists, on the other hand, find in the peculiar structure of the Sumerian language a link with that spoken by the "Turki" peoples of Western Central Asia, who are also of the broad-headed type. Others would go still farther afield to China in the east, to the Caucasus in the north and to the Bantu races of Africa in the west.

The discovery of a long-standing culture in the Indus Valley, with clay figurines showing a marked similarity to customs prevalent in the earliest days in Mesopotamia, certainly suggests some connection—possibly racial—between the two countries; and if so, it might have passed across Iran or through the coastal route of Baluchistan—perhaps by sea.(2)

That the people of the Second Period included members of a broad-headed race is acknowledged. Although not in a majority these may nevertheless have been the mainspring of their enterprise, the inspirers of their religion and the controlling element in the artistic and linguistic attainments which reveal themselves at this time in the history of Mesopotamia. The physical features of these men of Sumer or KI-EN-GI (the Land of the Reeds), as they called their country-land, can be judged from the representations left us in their seal impressions, their slab reliefs, their inlayed work, and their statues. Some had a high narrow head with rather broad nose and dark hair, whence their nickname "black-heads"; others were stouter, of medium stature, with wide heads and pronounced aquiline noses. We find that in some cases a beard was worn, but the upper lip was shaved, while the long hair was tied in a knot at the back of the head like that of the women. In other cases and usually later the whole head is shaved, probably in accordance with certain ritual observances. The men had skirts of sheepskin, full or short according to rank or office; the women wore short coats with tasselled or flounced skirts, probably of cloth, and a great deal of jewelry if wealthy (see Plates I and II).

With these theories and statements before us, we will now present further details of the geographical distribution of some of the earliest instruments used by the Sumerians, leaving the reader to judge how far music lends its support to the various views as to their origin, and at the same time remembering the important bearing which evidence of invention has on cultural affinity.

Of the three chief ritual instruments—the harp, the drum and the flute—we have already shown that the first two are distinctly Asiatic. They are so recognized by Dr Sachs in his *Geist und Werden der Musikinstrumente*. Both the bow-shaped harp and the hour-glass-shaped drum are traceable to Eastern Iran, India, Turkestan and Tibet. The harp appears in the Jemdet Nasr Period at the close of the fourth millennium B.C. It is ultimately superseded by the upright harp with its elevated sound-box. This type presents itself at Sippar at the opening of the second millennium B.C. and may have been introduced from Elam or the Iran plateau with which, as shown by the Niḥawend procession (*c.* 2200 B.C.) illustrated on Plate VI, 3, it was connected and at later times, as the Persian *chank*, so closely associated.

The vertical flute finds its earlier distribution also in Asia—western, central and eastern—to the shores of the Pacific Ocean. In Asiatic Turkey, Arabia, Bokhara, Persia, Baluchistan, Tibet, China, Burmah, India and Malaysia as well as in Mesopotamia it has not ceased to play its part. In India it is the Dravidian-speaking Todas who still maintain this primitive instrument of pre-Sanskrit days. The African flutes show a different development of the same principle.

The late arrival of the long-necked lute in the second millennium appears to be due to the incursion of Hittite or Amorite tribes from the west; or again, it may have been derived from the Mitannian influence on the north, for this type of instrument is linked with those of Aryan India—a culture with which at any rate the ruling class in Mitanni was racially associated.

The reed-blown pipes, both single and double with beating or clarinet-type reeds, appear in the Early Dynastic Period of Mesopotamia. But there is reason to believe that they were introduced from Egypt where they have held undisputed sway from the dawn of history. The pipe is represented on an archaic slate-palette, found at Hierakonpolis of Early First Dynasty date; here it is played by a jackal or a man so disguised. A small seated clay figure, from the same site, was evidently blowing a similar instrument, though it has now disappeared from his mouth. It was during this Early Dynastic Period, or perhaps even a little before, that commerce passed freely between the Sumerians and Egypt, though it seems to have been less towards the end of that time.

Of another early instrument, the lyre, we have already stated that it was probably found by the Sumerians in a primitive form when they reached their new land. It seems to be characteristically Semitic, as its adoption by the Hebrews for their national emblem would suggest. With it too we should probably class the sistrum, which in its peculiar "spur" form occurs in representations of the Early Dynastic and subsequent Agade Period of the third millennium B.C. We have previously given reasons for believing that it was not a gift from Egypt; its primitive association with the lyre and timbrel in worship as well as its later use in some form by the Jews appears to indicate a racial connection. Rattles and metal jingles of various kinds are widely distributed amongst the nations; but, so far as is known, this particular form of ritual rattle is not found eastward of Mesopotamia, though a primitive spur-type sistrum (*rau-rau*), with half cocoanut shells as "jingles", is used by Malay fishermen, perhaps introduced by early Arab traders.

The appearance of the "blowing" horn in the legendary story of the ancient Sumerian hero, Gilgamesh, is especially interesting. Though now so generally known in Africa, it is, as the late Dr E. von Hornbostel pointed out, lacking in Egypt. He considered that, in the "animal-horn" type, at any rate, it was a very early Hamitic instrument and introduced into Africa by an immigration across the Red Sea. In the Gilgamesh Epic, as has been fully explained in the second chapter, it is merely a hollow piece of wood—a branch with a larger attachment at the end to form a resonant bell. It was for a long time a pastoral instrument, like the wooden horns of hilly countries at the present day. It seems to have come from the upland districts of Asia and may have been introduced into Mesopotamia by the Sumerians, who evidently connected it with magical rites. The later forms, made in metal, are certainly associated with the Trans-caucasian and Anatolian districts.(3)

It is in the Early Dynastic Period, which immediately preceded the Agade or Sargonid rule of Semitic ascendancy, that we see these Sumerians in the full glory of their remarkable culture. Though communication had still been maintained with India through the Baluchistan highways, they had followed their own line of artistic development. With Northern Syria and the Caucasus they were in trading relationship; and as for Iran with its Elamite population, their near neighbours and ultimate vanquishers on the east, the Sumerians seem to have given to them more than they received from their somewhat slowly maturing civilization. Unfortunately with the increasing power of the Semitic Akkadians new ideas were introduced and different interests. That the rich land of the Two Rivers was ever open to invasion by envious tribes there can be no doubt; the history of the country is bound up with it. But the achievement of this wonderful people lies herein: that, notwithstanding attack from without and

PLATE XI. WIND INSTRUMENTS

1. Vertical Flute (*TIK*, *TEK* or *TI*), Ancient China
2. Vertical Flute, Ancient Egypt
3. Chinese Ocarina (*Hsüan*)
4. Reed-pipe in silver, from Ur; *c.* 2800 B.C.
5. Indian Pipe with "covered" reeds (*Tubri*)
6. Horn-pipe with "covered" reed, Greek Islands
7. Horn-pipe, Wales
8. Horn-pipe, China
9. Etruscan Bulb-pipes
10. Mediaeval Platerspiel or Bladder-pipe
11. Ambuba and Keraulos, Asia Minor
12. Syrian Pipe (*Suryānai*)
13. Arabian Bagpipe (*Gajda*)
14. Wooden Horn (bark-bound), East Finland
15. Persian Horn (*Buki*)
16. Tibetan Leg-bone Horn (*Kang-t'ung*)
17. Indian Horn (*Schringa*)
18. Gourd Trumpet, Uganda
19. Miniature Horns, Astrabad and Damghan, Persia; *c.* 1700 B.C.
20. Egyptian Trumpet, Medinet Habu; *c.* 1200 B.C.
21. Hittite Trumpet, Eyuk; *c.* 1000 B.C.
22. African Wooden Trumpet (natural branch)
23. Persian Trumpet (*Karana*)
24. Abyssinian Trumpet (*Malakat*)
25. Egyptian Trumpet; *c.* 1350 B.C.
26. Indian Trumpet (*Karna*)

PLATE XI

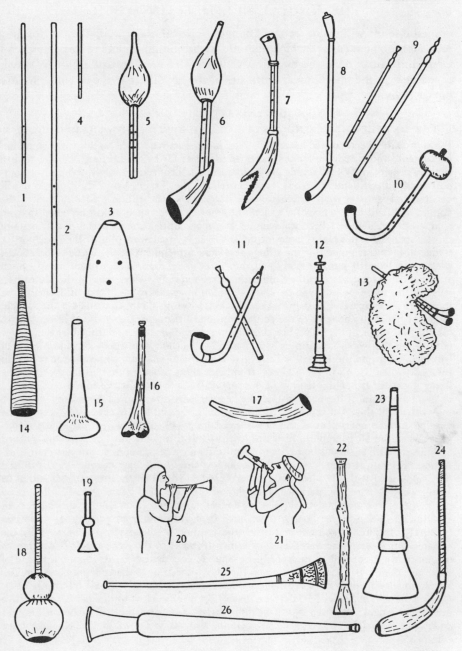

domestic feuds within, in spite of changes political and racial, they established on a high plane a culture which not only withstood the shocks of three thousand years, but imparted to the human race a knowledge of art and of order, which is reflected in the liberties and amenities of the far different age in which we are ourselves living.

ADDITIONAL NOTE ON

THE DEVELOPMENT AND DISTRIBUTION OF THE BOW-SHAPED HARP

It has probably been noticed how much stress has been already laid on this early Sumerian instrument; and rightly so, for the specimen found at Ur by Sir Leonard Woolley and so cleverly preserved by him stands pre-eminent for its beauty and rarity. When it is compared with the still more archaic type figured on the Bismya vase (Pl. V, 1, 2), it will be observed how far more elaborate and decorative it is; this is evidently due to the applied skill and experience of the men of Sumer. For instance, it will be noted that, in comparison with the earlier form, the neck is more upright, thus permitting the use of shorter strings for the higher notes of the scale; it is fitted with pins at the side, not for tuning-pegs but as guides for the strings and their attachment at the required point; the neck too is tenoned into the body and the whole instrument highly ornamented. Such an advance was not achieved in a moment. Here too may we say that, in the illustration given of this more perfect type on Plate V, 3, we have taken the liberty of departing, in some slight degree, from the shape which has been given to it in reconstruction, and which, no doubt, faithfully adheres to the actual position of the separated parts *as found*. About the size and shape of the sound-box there is no question, for it was outlined by the border of inlay, all the wood having perished. Beneath it nothing was discovered but a trace of corroded silver and some small nails. The point is, what was its true position in regard to the neck, when the harp was perfect? It appears most probable that, as the wood or the fixing decayed, either the tension of the remaining strings drew the sound-box upward or else the weight of the neck carried the heavier part downward. A rise from what we may call the "shoe" of the neck to the top of the sound-box is commonly seen in the existing African specimens of the bow-shaped harp (Pl. XII, 7, 8). But in the reconstruction of the Ur example, which was fractured at this point, the "step" is too marked and the sound-box should be brought down to its normal position, as shown in our illustration. Beneath it there was probably a shallow supporting base of solid wood, encased (it would seem) with silver plates to protect it, when rested on the ground. Moreover, as all the wooden parts had perished, the splay of the sides of the instrument, indicated by the shape of the terminal inlay, was no longer apparent. There must also have been sound-holes in the upper board; these have been outlined from present-day examples (Pl. XII, 7). This suggestion, as to the true position of the parts, is confirmed by the remains which were discovered of a second instrument of the same type. It was not so magnificently decorated as that of Queen Shubad just described; its mountings were of silver and there was no animal's head on the sound-chest; but it had copper pins or guides for fifteen instead of only eleven strings. The discoverer remarks, in his full *Report on the Ur Excavations* (vol. II, p. 167), that the lower pins were so close to the "shoe" as to leave insufficient length for the strings. This difficulty is obviated if the sound-chest is brought down and placed in its true relative position, such as is shown in the Khafage harp (Pl. V, 4).

We have spoken of the Sumerians as being possibly connected with the primitive Dravidian-speaking tribes of India. It is therefore interesting to observe that on buildings connected with the Buddhist religion, such as the *topes* with their railings at Sanchi and Amaravati in Central India, we have frequent representations of this bow-shaped harp, some with eleven strings (Pl. XII, 1). It is true that they are very much later than the period under our consideration; the earliest only dates from *c.* 100 B.C. But they take us back to a time anterior to the coming even of Brahminism (*c.* 1500 B.C.); for the instrument is plainly shown with three or four strings in the pictographs of the "Harappa" Indus Valley script (*c.* 2600 B.C.). Unrecorded in Sanskrit treatises, it was a folk-instrument of pre-Aryan date. On the sculptured slabs of Eastern Turkestan we find these same harps; and, as many authorities consider that the buildings of Central India are representative of a Bactrian or Eastern Iranian art, it is evident that such details as these connect them with the districts of Western Central Asia, which have already yielded rich traces of an early Sumerian culture. By the passage of this primitive harp through Southern Tibet, it reached Northern Burmah where we see it to-day (Pl. XII, 3); and, on the other hand, it spread northward to the Ugrian Ostyaks and, by the addition of a front pillar, became the parent of the European harp of Scandinavia (Pl. XII, 13, 14).

But we must turn southward again and recall the fact, which is becoming more and more evident, that the pre-dynastic Egyptians were indebted to this same Sumerian civilization for some of their knowledge in art and handicraft. Research has shown that Sumerian influence did not confine itself to Mesopotamia but passed on south-westward. Representatives of their race or races pursued their way through Arabia, probably by the Al-Batin and Darvasir Valleys (then amply supplied with water) to the southern end of the Red Sea, whence they crossed over the narrow outlet and reached what was afterwards known as Upper or Southern Egypt. Quite recently it has been discovered that the Badarians of Middle Egypt, the first true agriculturalists of the Nile Valley, not only show some resemblance to the negroids or to the races of Southern India, but knew also the use of copper, as the Sumerians did, though the prehistoric Egyptians did not. That the late pre-dynastic Egyptians had some sort of connection with the land of Sumer is evident. Here we find, pictured on tomb and temple walls or preserved in ancient graves, examples of this small bow-shaped harp (Pl. XII, 4, 6), and it is interesting to observe (as showing the persistence of early tradition) that, in the representation of the famous fleet of Queen Hatshepsut (*c.* 1492 B.C.) figured on the walls of the temple at Dêr el Bahri in Western Thebes, one of the ships has a bow-shaped harp with three strings hung on the cordage of the main-mast. For this voyage was made to the "Holy Land" of South Arabia and to Punt as a mission of peaceful intercourse and trade, with the little harp hoisted, it may be, as a signal of friendship and affinity.

But, as will be noticed, the manner of holding the instrument is different from the earliest method and the structure of the Egyptian instrument is not so primitive as that displayed on the Sumerian vase (Pl. V, 1, 2). It has the guide-pins for the strings, which we have noted in the later development, though they are here placed at the back of the neck of the harp in a position not so satisfactory for the free vibration of the strings as at the side. It is a step, at any rate, to the same end. When, however, we come to the XIIth Egyptian Dynasty (*c.* 2000 B.C.) we find that, although it is still bow-shaped and without a front pillar, it is a much larger instrument, always placed on a stand or resting on the ground when in use (Pl. XII, 5). This southern development reached its highest pitch in the great harps of Thebes with their elegant form and numerous strings—an elaboration unknown in Mesopotamia.

Yet the simple and primitive type remains still in the southern part of the Nile Valley, for in the five-stringed *Nanga* of Nubia we have its counterpart. Carried by Phoenician traders to the shores of Greece and Italy it appeared as the *Nabla* or *Nablium* (Pl. XII, 2). More remarkable, however, is the fact that it has travelled westward across Africa, borne thither by Nilotic tribes under the pressure of invasion and consequent migration. In the more distant provinces, such as Adamana and the Kameruns, we find it with six to ten strings and in construction more like the earlier type (Pl. XII, 7).

In the harp of the Fan Tribe (Pl. XII, 8) there is a peculiar extension of the body; to it is now braced the curved neck. It appears to be the relic of a time when this harp was played with the neck resting against the shoulder as in the large Sumerian and Egyptian harps. The usual African method of holding the ordinary instrument is with the neck forward and away from the player, as on the Bismya vase, and the Asiatic carvings. The guide-pins inserted into the side of the neck, as in the Sumerian harp, are here used also as tuning pegs; these side pegs mark it off from the common stringed instruments of the African continent, such as the popular Semitic lyre known as the *kissar*, which is gradually ousting the old harp. These are without tuning pegs, except in cases where Turkish or Moorish instruments have established themselves.

It may be perhaps objected that the African bow-shaped harp is a natural outcome of the musical bow, so commonly used throughout the whole of Southern Africa below the equator. In Northern Africa, however, this musical bow is unknown, and between the two districts the bow-shaped harp, in its developed form, is found and found only in a well-defined but narrow tract of country from east to west. Owing to its peculiar exclusiveness and manifest superiority over the primitive bow, we do not consider that it is indebted for its existence in Africa to the common instrument of the south. That musical bow seems to have had its own line of development on the continent of Africa through the *Wambee* or *Volga* to the *Bandju* or African psaltery, destitute of tuning pegs. The triangular Kru harp, popular around Sierra Leone, evidently owes its origin to the outside influence of another continent.

The *Kundi* or bow-shaped harp of Uganda with its oval-form body, often consisting of a tortoise shell, is giving way to the Busoga lyre. It is instructive to note, however, that a barbarous practice, which was in vogue amongst the Bantu-speaking Baganda (as the people of Uganda are called), once had its counterpart also among the Sumerians. For the valuable and prolific discoveries at Ur were largely due to a burial cult, which happily died out long ages ago. It was, however, still the custom in the Early Dynastic Period of the land of Sumer, that upon the death of a king or queen the servants of the royal household, guards, horsemen, dancing girls and even members of the harem, should gather together and put themselves to sleep with a narcotic poison in the open space outside the royal tomb. Their bodies were then laid around in order, with their weapons, carts, instruments of music and beautiful apparel in order that, according to their belief, they might minister to the needs of their deceased master or mistress in the shadowy and mysterious beyond. We will now quote from a description of the old burial customs in Uganda, performed only on the death of a king or queen. "When the hood [over the entrance of the tomb] was let down to close it, the wives of the late king, who had been bound, were placed at intervals round the tomb from the left of the doorway onwards and were clubbed to death; the men (viz. the chief cook, the chief brewer, the chief herdsman, the keeper of the king's well and the chief in ch..rge of the sacred fire) were clubbed to death on the right side of the door; these and hundreds more were killed and sent to attend upon the king, who was supposed to need them in the other world. None of their bodies were buried, but they were left where they fell around the tomb." And yet another point of similarity; amongst this African tribe there is a system of clans, dating from an unknown antiquity. One clan, claiming as their forefather the first king's great friend, who came to Uganda with him, is of lighter build than the rest and its members have fine "Roman" features. Could that forefather have had Sumerian blood as well as features? At any rate we are learning from East African archeological exploration that the earliest inhabitants of the district around the Great Lakes often had Asiatic characteristics and not those of the present-day African.

Of the derivatives of the bow-shaped harps two have been already described in the third chapter. The ɛšɪʀᴛᴜ or "ten-stringed" angle-harp appears to have undergone certain improvements, for it will be noticed that the illustration given on the Nippur plaque of the Ist Babylonian Dynasty (Pl. VI, 4) shows the strings grouped closely together towards the base of the upright rod. It may have been an artist's misconception of a newly introduced instrument, but it is certainly not so efficient from a musical standpoint as the later "spaced" stringing of the Assyrian Period (Pl. XII, 9). The upright harp or ᴢᴀᴋᴋᴀʟ, which became known as the Persian *chank*, and passed in the Middle Ages eastward to the north Pacific coast and westward to the Pillars of Hercules, is peculiarly a Western Asiatic development, being in its origin popular in Iran and Elam, as shown by examples from Niḥawand, at Malamir, and also from Egypt, though there in the later days its elevated sound-box lost the graceful curve of the Asiatic model and was "wooden-framed" (Pl. VI, 1) instead of "dug-out"; a stretched skin formed the sound-board.

We must probably consider this particular form of the harp as a by-product, for the modern type of instrument evidently is derived more directly from the bow-shaped harp of Central Asia, having been developed from an instrument which was held with the neck uppermost (Pl. V, 4, 5). A positive link moreover seems to have been found in the harp of the Ostyak tribes of Western Siberia on the Ob (Pl. XII, 13), who probably obtained their original instrument from Turkestan or some neighbouring district. It came to them without a front pillar or support, for we are assured by Dr Sachs that the instrument is complete without it. The small specimen (Pl. XII, 14), now in the Asiatic Ethnographical Collection at the British Museum, corroborates this statement; for the front support has been "sprung in" as an after-thought, preventing indeed the employment of the longest string. In *Instrumentenkunde*, Dr Heinitz illustrates a bow-shaped harp from the Caucasus with twelve strings and a stick for a front pillar. The Finns, racially connected with the Ostyaks and coming from Western Siberia into Europe in the seventh century of our era, brought this harp with them; and it is stated that the last player, who did not use the front pillar, died in Estonia about a century ago. It is to this migration we appear to owe the northern type of harp with its front pillar, often "bent" as in the Irish clarseth, which we have figured and fully described elsewhere. An Eastern Asiatic form of the bow-shaped harp, said to be Chinese but more probably Cambodian, shows a somewhat parallel attempt to overcome the defect of the unsupported curved neck (Pl. XII, 15). From such a humble origin has arisen that graceful and beautiful instrument, which, permeating the whole of Europe during the past thousand years, holds an honoured place in the finest orchestras of to-day.(4)

PLATE XII. STRINGED INSTRUMENTS

1. Indian Harp, Sanchi; *c.* 200 B.C.
2. Pompeian Harp (*Nablium*); *c.* 79 A.D.
3. Burmese Harp (*Saun*)
4. Egyptian Harp (*Ban*); *c.* 300 B.C.
5. Egyptian Upright Harp; *c.* 2000 B.C.
6. Egyptian Bow-shaped Harp; *c.* 1500 B.C.
7. African Harp, Adamana
8. African Harp (*Ombi*), Fan Tribe
9. Assyrian Horizontal Harp (*Eširtu*); c. 650 B.C.
10. Assyrian Upright Harp (*Zaḳḳal*); *c.* 650 B.C.
11. Chinese Harp (*K'ung-hou*); *c.* 600 A.D.
12. Moorish Harp; *c.* 1200 A.D.
13. Ostyak Harp, Western Siberia (*Torop-jux*)
14. Ostyak Harp, Western Siberia (*Torop-jux*)
15. Cambodian Harp, S.E. Asia

PLATE XII

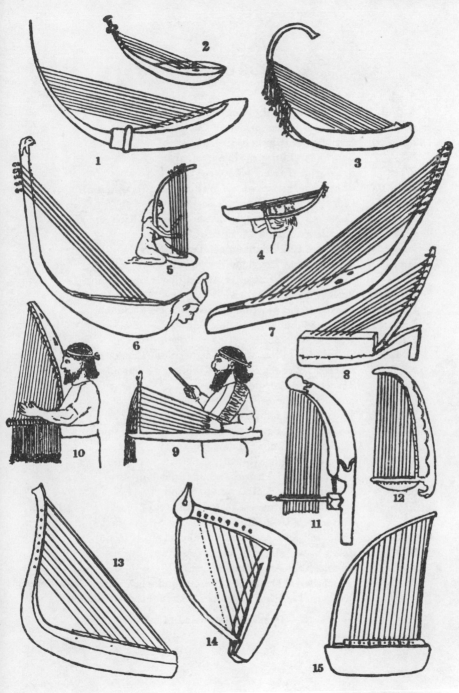

ABBREVIATIONS

A.J.L.	Antiquaries Journal (London Soc. of Antiquaries).
A.J.S.L.	American Journal of Semitic Languages.
A.O.	Archiv für Orientforschung (Berlin).
B.A.	Beiträge zur Assyriologie (Berlin).
B.L.	Babylonian Liturgies (Langdon, 1913).
B.T.	Babylonian Tablets (Clay, 1923).
C.I.	Cuneiform Inscriptions of Western Asia (Rawlinson).
C.O.I.	Chicago Oriental Institute Series.
C.T.	Cuneiform Texts in the British Museum (King, etc.).
E.M.	Encyclopédie de la Musique (Lavignac).
H.G.T.	Historical and Grammatical Texts (Poebel).
H.R.T.	Historical and Religious Texts (Langdon).
I.S.A.	Inscriptions des Sumer et Akkad (Thureau-Dangin).
J.A.	Journal Asiatique (Paris).
J.A.O.S.	Journal of the American Oriental Society (Boston).
J.R.A.S.	Journal of the Royal Asiatic Society (London).
J.S.A.L.	Journal of the Society of Arts (London).
P.M.A.	Proceedings of the Musical Association (London).
P.S.B.A.	Proceedings of the Society of Biblical Archaeology.
R.A.	Revue d'Assyriologie (Paris).
R.Ac.	Rituels Accadiens (Thureau-Dangin).
S.B.H.	Sumerian and Babylonian Hymns (Reisner).
S.B.P.	Sumerian and Babylonian Psalms (Langdon, 1909).
S.G.	Sumerian Grammar (Langdon, 1911).
S.H.	Sumerian Hymns (Radau).
S.L.P.	Sumerian Liturgies and Psalms (Langdon, 1919).
S.L.T.	Sumerian Liturgical Texts (Langdon, 1917).
S.R.T.	Sumerian Religious Texts (Chiera, 1924).
S.T.	Sumerian Tablets (Hussey, Harvard Semitic Series).
T.R.A.B.	Textes religieux Assyriens et Babyloniens (Martin).
U.D.T.	Ur Dynasty Tablets (Nies, 1920).
Z.A.	Zeitschrift für Assyriologie (Leipzig).
Z.D.M.G.	Zeitschrift der Deutschen Morgenländischen Gesellschaft (Leipzig).
Z.V.M.	Zeitschrift für Vergleichende Musikwissenschaft (Berlin).

(Other works quoted in full.)

REFERENCES AND NOTES

To avoid undue multiplication of text references, the notes are arranged under paragraphs, the reference number being placed at the end of the section and key-words given. For abbreviations used see previous page.

CHAPTER I

DRUMS, TIMBRELS AND RATTLES

1. Dancing sticks: Illustrated and described by Woolley, *Ur Excavations Report*, II (1934), p. 127, figs. 21–3; Legrain, *Ur Excavations*, III (1936), no. 384; Mackay, *A Sumerian Palace and the "A" Cemetery at Kish*, Part II, Chicago (1929), p. 160, pl. LXI.

2. UB (*uppu*), a drum: Thureau-Dangin, *Rituels Accadiens* (1921); Sidney Smith, R.A. XXI, p. 80; Genouillac, *Sumerian Hymns*, R.A. XXV, p. 154; Early ideograms: Barton, B.A. IX (*Origin of Babylonian Writing*), no. 376; Langdon, S.L.P. (1919), Tablet 13856 (1), obv. 23. UB-TUR: Scheil, R.A. XVII, p. 49. UB-ZABAR: Langdon, A.J.S.L. XXXIX, p. 171, l. 26. Chinese *happu*: Piggott, *Mus. Instruments of Japan*, p. 196. Processional use: Macmillan, B.A. v, p. 581.

3. BALAG, an hour-glass-shaped drum. Early ideogram: Deimel, *Liste der archaïschen Keilschriften*, no. 41; Barton, B.A. IX, nos. 309, 595. The illustration is of the Gudea Period (*c.* 2400 B.C.). BALAG-TUR: Scheil, R.A. XVII, p. 49. Of cedarwood: Reisner, *Tempelurkunden*, p. 112. "*Palagga*": Thureau-Dangin, *Rituels Accadiens*, p. 110.

4. "Perfect Music": *Gudea Cylinder*, B, XV, 20. "Assuaging tears": Chiera, S.R.T. Rev. VI, 14, 15. "Attract attention": Sayce, *Archiv für Orientforschung*, II, p. 106. Its use with the voice shown in such phrases as SÌR BALAGGA (*zamâr balaggi*) "to sing to the drum": BALAG ZÚRRATA (*ina balaggi u ikríbi*) "with drum and supplication".

5. Use of the BALAG: Dream of *Gudea Cyl.* A, VI, 24; the word SILIM, variously translated "soothing" or "pleasing", has the underlying meaning of prosperity or safety—hence "auspicious" or "propitious", "of good omen". Year dating: Thureau-Dangin, *Inscriptions des Sumer*, etc. p. 325. The transference of the name of an instrument to the musician, who plays it, is common in many languages; we speak, for instance, of a "First Violin" when we denote the performer. In the seventeenth century a Spanish trumpeter is described as "the Italian Trumpet" because he used this particular type of instrument (Pedrell, *Organografía musical antigua española*, p. 134).

6. Drum speech: Densmore, *Chippewa Music* (Bureau of American Ethnology, Bulletin 53, pp. 142 ff.); *Gudea Cyl.* A, VI, 24; Wallaschek, *Primitive Music*, p. 112; Rowbotham, *History of Music*, I, pp. 10 ff.; Wieschoff, *Die afrikanischen Trommeln* (1933); P. R. Kirby, *Mus. Instruments of the Native Races of S. Africa* (1934), pp. 36 ff.; C. Sachs, *Die Instrumente Indiens*, p. 75. Drum omens: A. Clay, B.T. XIII, p. 54. Sound of the drum: *Gudea Cyl.* A, XXVIII, 17; B.A. v, 667, 18. For further details of the hour-glass drum, cf. W. H. Ward, *Seal Cylinders of Western Asia* (Columbia Carnegie Institute, Washington), p. 361. European examples: Riaño, *Early Spanish Music* (1887), pp. 109, 111.

7. The circular head of the BALAG-DI is not only suggested by the Akkadian word, which is connected with *timbu* (a ring), but by the expression GIŠ GAM BALAG-DI (Akk. *kippat timbûti*) also applied to the BALAG and to the A-LA or large drum mentioned later. *Kippatu* denotes either a circular surface or the circumference (arc) of a circle: R.A. XXIX, p. 24, XXX, p. 187. Elamite seal from Susa: R.A. XXV, p. 175, fig. 1. Field cricket: Landsberger, *Die Fauna* (1934), p. 125. Friction drums: H. Balfour, *Royal Anthropological Institute Journal*, XXXVII (1907); P. R. Kirby, *Musical Instruments of S. Africa* (1934). *Ragāmu ša timbutti* "to make a noise like a cricket": Langdon, S.L.P. pp. 253 ff. For Lipushiau's appointment: Thureau-Dangin, *Inscript. des Sumer*, etc. p. 237. BALAG-LUL: Langdon, B.L. p. xxviii; S.G. p. 227; Reisner, S.B.H. 109, 74.

8. DUB: Muss. Ainolt (*Assyrian Dict.* p. 356) gives, as Akkadian, *timbúbi*. DUB with LUB (L):
A.J.S.L. XXIII, p. 148, l. 79. BALAG with seven-note flute: Langdon, A.J.S.L. XXXIX, pp. 161 ff.,
Hymn I, col. IV, 26: also B.L. p. xxxvii, liturgical note Fox Strangways, *Music of Hindostan*, p. 76,
"Music in its highest and most emblematic form moves to the sound of Krishna's Flute and
dances to the pulsations of Shiva's Drum."

9. Abstract use of words *balag*, etc.: D. Macmillan, B.A. v, p. 581; *Cuneiform Texts from Babylonian Tablets* (B.M.), XII, col. I, 20; Rawlinson, *Cuneiform Inscript. of Western Asia*, II, 49, no. 5,
ob. 7; Thureau-Dangin, *Inscript. des Sumer*, etc. p. 106, note.

10. A-LA: *Gudea Cyl.* A, col. XVIII, 19, XXVIII, 18; B, XV, 20, XIX, I. SU A-LA: P.S.B.A. (1911),
p. 186; A.J.S.L. XXXIX, pp. 161 ff., Hymn I, col. III, 25; Langdon, S.L.P. p. 249, l. 23. We
consider that the A-LA (or A-LAL) ZABAR and the URUDU A-LA, listed among metal objects in
the store-room of the temple in Girsu by M. Hussey (*Sumerian Tablets*, Part II, p. 3) and Reisner
(*Tempelurkunden*, no. 126) and stated by Chiera (S.R.T.) to be drums, are more probably bronze
and copper vessels for libations or sacrificial purposes. A-LA in Lagash Temple: *Gudea Cyl.*
B, XIX, I (Price reads *ud-dam múr mu-na-ab-gé* "rage like the storm": Thureau-Dangin reads
ud-dam síg mu-na-ab-gí "briller comme le jour", translating A-LA as "cymbals"). NIN-AN-DA-
GAL-KI: Thureau-Dangin, *Gudea Statue*, E, col. IV, 12–14, col. V, I. Illustrations of A-LA: G. Cros,
Nouvelles fouilles de Tello (1905–9), pl. IX, fig. 4; R.A. IX, pl. III (with figure of Ea); A.J. (London),
V, pl. XLVI (Ur-Nammu Stele). SU GU-GALU: Langdon, S.L.P. p. 339. Egyptian drum: Lavignac,
E.M. I, 13. Hittite drum (and horn): *Brit. Mus. Report Carchemish*, II. Offerings: Genouillac,
Inventaire des Tablets, Part II, no. 833. Chinese "hanging" drums: A. C. Moule, J.R.A.S. (North
China Branch), XXXIX. Indian examples: C. Sachs, *Die Musikinstrumente Indiens*, p. 75.

11. LILIS, a kettledrum: Thureau-Dangin, *Rituels Accadiens*, A.O. 6479; Langdon, B.L. pp.
xii ff. For tablet illustration: R.A. XVI, p. 145 and notes; Yetts, *Eumorfopoulos Collection Cat.*
II, pp. 13 ff. Egyptian hand-drum: Engel, *Music of the Most Ancient Nations*, fig. 64. Eclipse and
omen ritual: A. Clay, *Bab. Tablets* (Morgan), nos. 6 and 13. Except for the *balag* type of drum
we have at present failed to find any of the double-headed instruments of barrel shape so frequently shown on Egyptian wall-paintings and represented in the Indian drums of the present
day.

12. A-DÂPA as a grain measure: Thureau-Dangin, J.S.A. Series X, vol. 13 (1909), p. 84.
Ceremonial use: Chiera, S.R.T. (1924), no. 12; Langdon, J.R.A.S. (1921), *Babylonian and Hebrew
Musical Terms*, p. 171; A.J.S.L. XXIX, p. 179. Elamite illustration: J. de Morgan, *Mémoires
de la Délégation en Perse*, vol. III, Series I, pl. 23. Louvre seal: L. Delaporte, *Cylinder Seals in Louvre*,
I, pl. LI, 22. "Muscovite" type: Praetorius, *Syntagma Musicum*, II, pl. XXX, 3. Niḥawand illus-
tration: E. Herzfeld, *Schweich Lectures*, London (1934).

13. ME-ZE: with A-DÂPA, J.R.A.S. (1921), p. 171. SU ME-ZE, Langdon, B.L. p. xxxii;
S.G. p. 52. ME-ZI-MA, Langdon, S.B.P. p. 128 and B.L. 79, 17; Reisner, *Hymnen*, Introd. p. xvii,
no. 72, rev. 10; Macmillan, B.A. v, p. 581. Illustrations from Kish: Genouillac, *Kish*, II, pl. III.
Tell Halaf: Oppenheim, *Tell Halaf*, pp. 120 and 179. Kassite: Délégation en Perse, *Mém.*
VII, pls. 27, 28; also A. Jeremias, *Das alte Testament* (1930), p. 501. Ur (remains): *Ur Excavation
Report*, II, p. 157. For mediaeval use of Duff and Ghirbal: H. G. Farmer, *History of Arabian Music*,
pp. xiv, 28, 52–53; *Studies in Oriental Mus. Instruments*, p. 84; E. Mackay, *Indus Civilization*, p. 184.

14. Egyptian *sistra*: C. Sachs, *Die Musikinstrumente des alten Ägyptens* (1921); also *Musik des
Altertums* (1924), p. 15. Agade seal: L. Delaporte, *Cylinder Seals in the Louvre*, II, pl. 74, 1 (A 172);
Messant, *Glyptiques*, II, fig. 100. Ur Sistrum: *Excavations Report*, II, p. 261, pl. 221.

15. Legal code on KATRAL: F. Hrozny, *Code Hittite*, p. 116. "Katras" woman: *Archiv für
Orientforschung*, II, p. 106. Egyptian cymbals: Carl Sachs, *Die Musikinstrumente des alten Ägyptens*
(1921). Tell Halaf relief: Oppenheim, *Tell Halaf*, p. 179. Indian cymbals: C. Sachs, *Die
Musikinstrumente Indiens*. p. 19; C. R. Day, *Music of S. India*, pl. XIII.

16. Bronze Bells in British Museum: Engel, *Music of the Most Ancient Nations*, p. 65. NIG-
KAL-GA: Langdon, S.L.P. p. 339; Jastrow, *Bildermappe zur Religion Babyloniens*, figs. 70 and 70 a.
Bells in Mithraic ceremonies: F. Cumont, *The Mysteries of Mithra*, p. 166. Chinese temple bells:
Van Aalst, *Chinese Music*, pp. 52–75.

CHAPTER II

FLUTES, PIPES AND HORNS

1. TI-GI, a vertical flute: *Gudea Cyl.* B, IX, 9 ff. KA-GI: Chiera, S.R.T. no. 14, ob. 20. IMIN-E, Eridu tablet: A.J.S.L. XXXIX, p. 161, no. 1, col. II, 33, IV, 26; Chiera, S.R.T. no. 8, ob. col. II, 24. GI-GID: Langdon, S.L.T. p. 140, l. 56. GI-BU: Craig, R.T. pl. XV, 6. GIŠ-SÍR: Rawlinson, *Cun. Inscript. of Western Asia*, II, 22, no. 1. GI-DIM: Rawlinson, *l.c.* II, 45, no. 1, 3. LUB-DUB-TA: A.J.S.L. XXIII, p. 148, l. 79.

2. Vertical flute and pan-pipes: C. Sachs, *Die Musikinstrumente des alten Ägyptens* (1921); Chappell, *History of Music*, p. 65. Hierakonpolis tablet: Quibell and Green, *Hierakonpolis*, II, pl. 28. Louvre seal: Lajard, *Introd. à l'histoire du culte de Mithra*, pl. XLI, 5. The invention of the Monaulos was attributed to Pan by Pliny, *Hist. Nat.* VII, 56.

3. Birs Nimrûd whistle: Engel, *Music of the Most Ancient Nations*, pp. 75 ff.; C. K. Wead, *History of Musical Scales* (Report Smithsonian Inst. U.S.A. Museum, 1900), p. 431. Bantu whistles: Ankermann, *Die afrikanischen Musikinstrumente*, pp. 36 ff. A large number of bone whistles have been recently discovered with palaeolithic remains at Vestonice, Moravia, by Dr K. Absolon (see *Illustrated London News*, March 28, 1936). P. R. Kirby, *The Musical Instruments of the Native Races of S. Africa*, pp. 106 ff., pl. XXXIX (b). Chinese *Hsüan*: A. C. Moule, J.R.A.S. (North China Branch), XXXIX, p. 61. [The scale given should be c^1, d^1 (lip notes), e^1, f sharp^1, g^1, a^1, b^1, c^2, corresponding to the ancient scale of the YO or TI, cf. note 2 chap. IV. The Gawra prehistoric bone (*Am. Sch. Orient. Research*, 1936) is a double-whistle-pitch b^3.

4. Ishtar Epic: Langdon, R.A. XII, pp. 73 ff.; Sidney Smith, R.A. XXX, p. 163. Note the ideograms RA ("to strike") used of sound effect; BAR ("to be high", "to rise") intensified by reduplication. Bantu *uku*: Kirby, *Mus. Inst. S. Africa*, pp. 82, 96, 98. The Kirghis *Čor*—now merely a childish toy—with two notes, has no whistle-head and is more primitive than the form found in Turkestan. The African *naka* (Kirby, *l.c.* p. 97, pl. XXXIV) is a stopped tube like the Assyrian UKU. For Chinese whistle, cf. Moule, J.R.A.S. (North China Branch), XXXIX, p. 71. Ocarina: Welch, *Lectures on the Recorder*, p. 344, n. 1; E. Mackay, *Indus Civilization*, p. 178.

5. Reed-pipe (single). Ur seal: *Ur Excavations Report*, II, p. 336, no. 12 and pl. 192. Early example: Lajard, *Culte de Mithra*, pl. XXIX, 7. Ishtar hymn: Craig, R.T. pl. 15, l. 6, "ḫalilu". GI-ER-RA: Rawlinson, *Cun. Inscrip. of Western Asia*, IV, nos. 11, 27 and 28a. Enlil Liturgy: Langdon, S.L.T. X, p. 161, col. II, 14; Chaucer, *House of Fame*, III, 135. GIŠ GÙ SÌR: Langdon, S.G. p. 199, l. 58. NÁ: F. Martin, T.R.A.B. (1900), p. 39. Lamentation for Tammuz by Ishtar, l. 1: Nies and Keiser, *Babylonian Inscriptions*, p. 44. Ḫalil: Stainer, *Music of the Bible* (1914), p. 101.

6. Reed-pipe (double): Ur specimen (provisional description), Woolley, *Ur Excavations Report*, II, p. 258. Through the courtesy of Dr Legrain of the University Museum, Philadelphia, we have obtained full details and measurements of these interesting specimens of the double-pipe, the earliest at present known. They are given with other pipe measurements in the notes to Chapter I.. Leyden pipes: Lavignac, *Encyclopédie de la Musique*, Part I, p. 18 and note 2. Lady Maket pipes: Lavignac, *l.c.* pp. 20, 12 bis and 13 bis; T. L. Southgate, P.M.A. Session XVII, p. 13; Hermann Smith, *World's Earliest Music*, pp. 25 ff. Nippur figurine: Legrain, *Terracottas from Nippur*, 1930. An interesting account of the growing and making of the single-beating reeds for these pipes is given by Theophrastus, *Hist. Plantarum*, IV, 11, 3–7 (a special translation in A. Hort's *Enquiry into Plants*, 1916).

7. ER-ŠEM-MA: Reisner, *Hymnen* (1896), Introd. xvii, no. 22 and no. 53; Langdon, S.B.P. p. 317; Macmillan, B.A. V, p. 581. Eclipse tablet: A. Clay, *Bab. Tablets (Morgan Coll.)*, no. 6. Foundation Ritual: Weissbach, *Misc.* XII, 12; cf. also Elamite Festal Orchestra (Pl. VI, 8) and Nimrûd ivory (Pl. VIII, 5). Sardinian Launedda: Riano, *Early Spanish Music*, fig. 45, no. 1; Mahillon, *Catalogue Mus. Instrumental*, Brussels, IV, 23.

8. KITMU ("covered" pipe): Langdon, J.R.A.S. (1921), p. 184. KANZABU: Macmillan, C.T., B.A. V, p. 566. Subulo pipes: Hermann Smith, *World's Earliest Music*, chs. V and IX; Southgate, P.M.A. Session XVII, p. 197. Pibgorn: H. Balfour, *Old British Pibcorn and its Affinities*

(1890); Galpin, *Old English Instruments*, p. 171. Chinese Pibgorn: Moule, J.R.A.S. (North China Branch), XXXIX, p. 85 and pl. IV, 3; Lavignac, *Encycl. Musique*, Part I, p. 159.

9. PITU ("crooked" pipe): Sidney Smith, R.A. xxx, p. 167. Susian figurine: J. de Morgan, *Délégation en Perse*, I, pl. VIII, 10, 14. Hittite bagpipe (?): Garstang, *Land of the Hittites*, 1910; Schlesinger, *Precursors of the Violin Family*, II, Frontispiece. GI-DI (*takaltu*): *Cuneiform Texts in Brit. Mus.* XVIII, pl. 34, vol. III, 25; Langdon, B.L. p. xxxiii; Zimmern, *Rit Tafeln*, 116, 117 on a tablet drawn up by order of Ashurbanipal (668–626 B.C.) for the royal library at Nineveh. For the reeds used see notes to Chapter IV, 4.

10. IMBUBU (MALILU), a double-beating reed pipe of the oboe type: Macmillan, B.A. v, p. 566. *Gingira*: Barton, B.A. IX, nos. 553 and 384. Ishtar Epic: R.A. xxx, p. 163. Hittite pipes: *Carchemish*, Brit. Mus. Report, II. Cypriote pipes: Perrot-Chipiez, *Histoire de l'Art*, III, p. 781. "Abôbas and Gingras": Lavignac, *Encycl. de la Musique*, I, p. 56. Tammuz Hymn: F. A. Vanderburgh, *Sumerian Hymns*, p. 18. Mediaeval history: Galpin, *Old English Instruments*, ch. IX.

11. Trumpets and horns: C. Sachs, *Die Musikinstrumente des alten Ägyptens* (1921); A. Hammerich, *Les Lurs*, Mém. de la Société Royale des Antiquités du Nord, Copenhagen (1892); T. Wilson, *Prehistoric Art*, U.S. Nat. Mus. Report (1896). Mari horns: *Syria*, XVI, pl. 21.

12. Gilgamesh Epic: C. J. Gadd, *The Epic of Gilgamesh Tablet* (XII, U 9364), R.A. xxx, pp. 127ff.; Sidney Smith, *b/pukk/qqu and mekku*, R.A. xxx, pp. 153ff.; Langdon, *Historical and Religious Texts*, B.E. XXXI, no. 55; Albert Schott, *Das Gilgamesch-Epos*, Leipzig (1934). The root BUK may be akin to PUK "to strike", used like the Hebrew and Arabic *taka* and the German *Stoszen* for sounding a trumpet; cf. Korean *Puk* (trumpet), Croatian *Buča*, Roman *Bucina*, Swiss *Büchel*, English *Bugle*. Arabian *buq*: Farmer, *History of Arabian Music*, p. 154. *Malakat*: a straight form is also found in Abyssinia. Bent, *Sacred City of Ethiopia* (p. 27). *Icilongo*: P. R. Kirby, *Mus. Insts. of S. Africa*, p. 80. Sassanian dish: O. M. Dalton, *Treasures of the Oxus*, p. 190. In Burmah and Assam: C. Sachs, *Die Musikinstrumente Birmas und Assams* (1917); also his *Lituus und Karnyx*, Liliencron Festschrift, Leipzig (1910), pp. 241 ff.

13. SI-IM (SÎM): *Gudea Cyl.* A, XVIII, 19, XXVIII, 18; B, XV, 20. The words SÎM and SÎM-DA have received various translations, Thureau-Dangin, uniting them with A-LA, rendering them "cymbals". A-LA, however, as a musical instrument, has its own determinative SU and is evidently a drum (see Chapter I, Section (a)). Price considers them as "cymbals" or as "horns"; Nies, rejecting "cymbals", translates "horn with breath", i.e. blowing horn, which, as it is the most natural interpretation and supported by ethnographical analogy and historical evidence, we have here adopted. Reisner, *Tempelurkunden* (1901), no. 124 and no. 279; Nies, *Ur Dynasty Tablets*, no. 1. SÎM "to call": Delitsch, *Sumerisches Glossar*, p. 247. *Şaddu*: Sidney Smith, l.c. p. 154. For temple receipts: Reisner, *supra*. SÎM of gold: Thureau-Dangin, *Tablettes Chaldiennes*, 221, obv. 1, 4; 223, obv. 1, 3. Hittite relief: *Carchemish*, Brit. Mus. Report, II. GI-SAL, Eridu tablet: Langdon, A.J.S.L. XXXIX, p. 164, l. 15. The supposed trumpet on a Babylonian seal (c. 2000 B.C.) is more probably a torch.

14. KARAN. Dušratta letters: Knudzton, *El Amarna Tablets*, pp. 155ff., no. 22, col. I, 36, II, 54, III, 45; no. 25, col. III, 37. Hittite relief, Ujuk: Pélagaud (Lavignac, *Encyl. Musique*, Part I, p. 53) considers this "un exemplaire de petite flûte"! It is evidently intended for the short trumpet as shown by the large bell. Miniature trumpets: Bode, *Treasure of Astrabad*, Archaeologia, xxx, pp. 248, 250, pl. XVI; S. Reinach, *Revue d'Archéologie* (1900), Paris, p. 58, figs. 72–82. Tepe Hissar Excavations: *Pennsylvania Museum Journal*, no. 4 (1933), pls. 124, 125. LABBANATU: Sennacherib's siege: Haupt, B.A. v, p. 594. Tut-ankh-amen trumpets: Howard Carter, *Tomb of Tut-ankh-amen*, II, pp. 19, 30. Dr Engelbach, Keeper of the Egyptian Museum, Cairo, has kindly supplied the following details: silver trumpet, length 22⅞ in. (0·582 m.); bronze trumpet, length 19⅞ in. (0·505 m.); in both specimens diameter of bell 3¼ in. (0·085 m.); of small end ½ in. (0·015 m.). There is no cup mouthpiece, but the tube terminates in a thickish metal ring on which it is difficult to produce sounds; the mouthpieces may be missing. The slight bend on the tube of the silver trumpet is due to age or accident. Early Egyptian trumpets (so-called): Lepsius, *Denkmaler*, Ab. II, pls. 27, 30.

15. CONCH (shell): Engel, *Music of the Most Ancient Nations*, p. 78; Sachs, *Die Musikinstrumente Indiens*, pp. 168 ff.; Mead, *Musical Instruments of the Incas* (American Museum of Nat. History, vol. III, Supplement 1903); Monograph by H. J. Brockelman, New Orleans (in preparation). Sanchi: Ferguson, *Tree and Serpent Worship*, on eastern gateway, first century A.D.

CHAPTER III

HARPS, LYRES AND LUTE

1. Sumerian harps: Woolley, *Ur Excavations Report*, II, pp. 249 ff. ZAG-SAL: Genouillac, *Note on Sumerian Hymns*, R.A. XXV, pp. 155 ff.; Zimmern, *Vergött. Lipit-Ishtar*, pp. 6 and 7, no. 6; Scheil, R.A. XXIII, p. 39; Rawlinson, *Cun. Inscriptions of Western Asia*, II, 26, ob. 27.

2. The AL tablet: Langdon, S.L.T. p. 187. In col. I, line 14, read "giš al-la-ni-ba tál-ba engur zagin-kam". Note at end: "giš al giš zag-sal dúg-ga". Decorated with gold: Scheil, R.A. XXIII, p. 39. "Great great ZAG-SAL": Chiera, S.R.T. no. 14, ob. 20. The remains of the second harp: *Ur Excavations Report*, II, p. 167, fig. 43. "ZAG-SAL" and flute (KA-GI): Chiera, S.R.T. no. 14, ob. 20. Large bow-harp (neck inward): *Ur Report*, III, fig. 369; on knee, fig. 373.

3. Eridu tablet: A.J.S.L. XXXIX, no. 1, col. 2, lines 28, 29. GIŠ-RU: Delitsch, *Sumerisches Glossar*, p. 178: *pitpanu* is now read *tilpanu*; *Gudea Cyl.* B, col. x, 11, "algar miri". Banks, *Bismya*, p. 267 f. Stone votive slabs: Frankfort, *Tell Asmar and Khafage*, C.O.I. XIII, p. 96. *Illustrated London News*, 9 June 1934, 14 Sept. 1935. Ur Seal: *Report*, III, p. 35. Coomaraswamy, J.A.O.S. 50, pp. 244–53, and 51, pp. 47 ff.; Lachmann, *Zeitschrift für Vergleichende Musikwissenschaft*, II, 57; Fox Strangways (Grove, *Dict. of Music*, s.v. *Indian Music*). "Saptatantri or seven-stringed vina": this can scarcely refer to the seven-stringed bow-harp (MIRITU), though the present Indian vina has seven strings (four on the finger-board and three as drones by the side), as Dr Coomaraswamy notes.

4. HUL: Barton, *Origin of Babylonian Writing*, B.A. IX, no. 495. It may be that the shape of the ZAKKAL was more convenient for processional use owing to the right-angled string attachment. Sippar figurine: Scheil, *Une Saison de fouilles à Sippar*, p. 90, fig. 2. Nihawand harp: E. Herzfeld, *Schweich Lectures*, London, 1934. Babylonian tablet: Sayce, *Hibbert Lectures*, p. 314, and P.S.B.A. XVII, pp. 133 ff. Esarhaddon at Nineveh: H. Winkler, *Esarhaddon. Changal, Chank*: H. Ravely, *Pushto Dictionary* 1867; Gesenius, *Heb. Lexicon*, p. 523; C. Sachs, *Die Musikinstrumente Indiens*, p. 141; H. G. Farmer, *History of Arabian Music*, p. 16. Berlin ZAKKAL: Sachs, *Zeitschrift für Ägyptische Sprache*, LXIX, pp. 68 f. Louvre ZAKKAL: Loret (Lavignac, *Encyclopédie de la Musique*, Part I), p. 29. Notwithstanding Loret's statement, twenty-one strings only should be allotted to this instrument, which is frequently depicted in an inverted position. It is correctly shown by Hortense Panum, *Middelalderens Strengeinstrumente*, Copenhagen (1915), p. 66. Illustrations: Naville (Lepsius, *Denkmäler*, II), p. 240; N. de Garis Davies, *El Amarna*, Part VI, pl. XXVIII—especially associated with Syrian women; R. Ker Porter, *Travels in Georgia, Persia*, etc. Egyptian statuette (B.M.): Stainer, *Music of the Bible* (1914), pl. V and notes. Cypriote and Greek examples in B.M.: Turkish harp: Engel, *Mus. Instruments in S. Kensington Museum*, p. 59. Moorish: Riano, *Early Spanish Music*, fig. 52. Egyptian upright harps: Engel, *Music of the Most Ancient Nations*, pp. 182–4. Duchesne-Guillemin, *La Harpe en Asie occidentale ancienne* (R.A. XXXIV, 1937).

5. ESIRTU (ten-stringed triangular harp): Langdon, *Babylonian and Hebrew Musical Terms*, J.R.A.S. (1921), p. 183; Stainer, *Music of the Bible* (1914), p. 42. The Egyptian specimen at Florence has been incorrectly strung: the hole at the broader end of the sound-box is for the carrying cord which, passing over the right shoulder of the player, was affixed to the front block. The illustration shows it rightly restored.

6. Lyres: Woolley, *Ur Excavations Report*, pp. 252 ff. Tell Halaf lyre: Oppenheim, *Tell Halaf*, pl. 38 and pp. 120, 181. Larsa lyre: Parrot, *Les fouilles de Tello et Larsa*, R.A. XXX, p. 169. Simpler form: B.M. Assyrian Saloon, slab 14 (Stainer, *Music of the Bible*, fig. 13). Eridu tablet (ZAG-SAL and AL-GAR): A.J.S.L. XXXIX, p. 161, col. II, 28, 32, and col. IV, 26. *Crotta*: Galpin, *Old English Instruments*, pp. 3 ff. Elamite seal: Legrain, *Culture of the Babylonians* (Bab. Section,

Pennsylvania Univ. xiv), no. 627. *Kinnor*: Stainer, *Music of the Bible*, ch. I, figs. 43–5. Beni-Hasan lyre: Wilkinson, *Manners and Customs of the Ancient Egyptians*, II, p. 296. El Amarna lyre: N. de Garis Davies, *El Amarna*, Part III, pl. 5, VI, pls. 6, 28. Lagash lyre: de Sarzec, *Découvertes en Chaldée*, pl. 23. Fara seal: Herzfeld, *Fara* (Archaeolog. Mitteilungen aus Iran, v), p. 75. Abyssinian lyre: Ankermann, *Die afrikanischen Musikinstrumente*, p. 23 and fig. 36. This type, with tuning rods, is also found in Somaliland. For the distribution of the lyre in Europe cf. Guillemin and Duchesne, *L'Antiquité classique*, IV, I (1935); T. Norlind, *Lyra und Kithara*, Stockholm (1934).

7. Ishtar Hymn: Langdon, S.G. p. 199, l. 59. Radau, *Miscell.* no. 2, rev. 59; *Gudea Cyl.* B, col. x, 11. Egyptian lyre in procession: Engel, *Music of the Most Ancient Nations*, p. 241. On Abyssinian lyre is the following inscription: "Qadmil (Kadmiel), son of —— asked the Trinity for help against the Gallas"; so provisionally read by Professor Margoliouth.

8. *SABITU* (seven-stringed lyre), Eridu tablet: A.J.S.L. XXXIX, p. 161, col. II, 29. Hymn to Nanâ: Macmillan, B.A. no. v, p. 56€. *Sebᵉka*: Dalman, *Aramaische Grammatik* (1905); Levias, *Aramaic Idiom* (1900); Gesenius, *Heb. Dict.* p. 597. A similar change to the harder guttural sound appears in *shemak* for *shama*, *areka* for *ara*, *makasah* for *maasah*, etc. *Sambuca*: Athenaeus, book XIV, ch. 33, quoting Andreas of Panormo. Crot or Rote: Galpin, *Old English Instruments of Music*, ch. I.

9. Lute type: H. Balfour, *Nat. History of the Musical Bow* (1899); P. R. Kirby, *Musical Instruments of S. Africa* (1934); C. Sachs, *Die Musikinstrumente Indiens*. Nefer: Sachs, *Die Musikinstrumente des alten Ägyptens* (1921); Stainer, *Music of the Bible* (1914), p. 45, note 2. Şinnitu: Macmillan, B.A. no. v, p. 566. Kish figurines: Genouillac, *Kish*, II, pl. 3. Hittite relief: J. Garstang, *Land of the Hittites*, p. 260, pl. 73; N. de Garis Davies, *El Amarna*, Part VI, pl. 28 (associated with Syrian women). Nippur plaque: Legrain, *Terracottas from Nippur*, fig. 94. Kassite seal: Delaporte, *Cylinder Seals in the Louvre*, pl. LI, no. 22.

10. Pandoura, Sumerian and Georgian: M. Tseretheli, J.R.A.S., 1913–16; cf. KI-EL-TUR, Georgian *qultuli* (young woman); Pollux, *Onomasticon*, IV, 60. In Arabia: Farmer, *Hist. of Arabian Music*, pp. 6ff. Babylonian *Kudurru*: Délégation en Perse, *Mémoires*, VII, pls. 27, 28; A. Jeremias, *Das alte Testament* (1930), p. 50 and *Gudea Cyl.* B, XII, 3, 4. For mediaeval history: E. Biernath, *Die Guitarre* (1907).

11. Psaltery, Chinese psalteries: A. C. Moule, J.R.A.S. (North China Branch), XXXIX, pp. 106ff.: Van Aalst, *Chinese Music*, pp. 59ff. For mediaeval shapes: Riano, *Early Spanish Music*; Galpin, *Old English Instruments*, pp. 56ff. Ishtar tablet: A.J.S.L. XXIII, p. 148, l. 71, (Reisner, no. 56) by M. Hussey. *Katyayana vina*: C. Sachs, *Die Musikinstrumente Indiens*, pp. 104 and 178.

MEASUREMENTS OF HARPS AND LYRES

Queen Shubad's harp (ZAG-SAL), Pl. V, 3	Height 3 ft. 6⅛ in. (1·07 m.). Length 3 ft. (0·915 m.). Max. width sound-board 5 in. (0·128 m.)
Upright harp (*ZAḲḲAL*), Musikinstr. Mus., Berlin, Pl. VI, 1, 2	Height 3 ft. 11½ in. (1·21 m.). Max. width sound-board 6¼ in. (0·16 m.)
Upright harp (*ZAḲḲAL*), Louvre, Paris	Height 3 ft. 8¼ in. (1·125 m.). Max. width sound-board 10½ in. (0·27 m.)
Ten-stringed harp (*EŠIRTU*), Florence, Pl. VI, 5	Height 1 ft. 2⅝ in. (0·37 m.). Length 1 ft. 9⅝ in. (0·55 m.). Max. width sound-board 3½ in. (0·09 m.)
Gold lyre (AL-GAR), Ur, Pl. VII, 1	Height 3 ft. 11¼ in. (1·20 m.)
Silver lyre (AL-GAR), Ur, Pl. VII, 3	Height 3 ft. 5¾ in (1·06 m.)
Boat-shaped lyre (*SABITU?*), Ur, Pl. VII, 2	Height 3 ft. 9⅝ in. (1·16 m.)

CHAPTER IV

SCALE AND NOTATION

1. For Dr Sach's paper on the Berlin Tablet (KAR. 1, 4) see note 7 *infra*.

2. Tsai Yü, *Lü Lü Ching I* (1596); cf. Moule, *Musical Instruments of the Chinese*, J.R.A.S. (North China Branch), xxxix, pp. 63, 71, 151; Amiot, *Mémoire sur la Musique des Chinois* (1779), pp. 160 ff.; Van Aalst, *Chinese Music* (1884); Courant, *La Musique classique des Chinois* (Lavignac, *Encyclop. de la Musique*, Part 1); *China Review*, 1, pp. 324–84; 11, pp. 47 f., 257 f. (scale of the sharp fourth). Description and measurements of the ancient YO or TI, as given by Tsai Yü (*Lü Lü Ching I*, IV, f. 17), are as follows: with all the holes closed the instrument gave *Kung* (D) or blown harder *Chih* (A); with the lowest hole open *Shang* (E) and *Yü* (B); with the two lower holes open *Chiao* (F♯) and *Ho* (C♯); and with the upper and lower holes open blown gently *Chung* (G). It will be noticed that Tsai Yü gives the scale according to the use of his own day and has attempted (without success) to make the "fourth" (G) perfect by cross-fingering: the natural scale (i.e. with all the three holes open) gives *Pien chih* (G♯) in agreement with the ancient scale and the *lüs*. The scale as given in the text has been set a whole tone lower to simplify reference, *Kung* being taken as C instead of D. For the theory of "blown fifths", cf. E. Hornbostel in *Handbuch der Physik*, VIII, pp. 425–49 (Berlin). With reference to the use of the sharp "fourth" Louis Spohr (*Selbstbiographie*, I, p. 257) remarks that "the country people sing the 'third' rather sharp, the 'fourth' *decidedly* sharp and the 'seventh' flat. It is the tone scale given us by nature, like the notes of a brass instrument untempered by the hand". It is interesting to note that in Java the seven-note "tritone" scale has been grafted into their ancient Erythrean pentatonic scale DE-GAB-D: for the scale *pelog* consists of D-E♭FGAB♭CD, cf. Land, *Über die Tonkunst der Javanen*.

Following Loret's system, as given in Lavignac's *Encylp. Mus.* Part I, p. 17, etc., the measurements of Tsai Yü's specimen are as follows:

Total length 20 inches (0·508 m.): internal diameter ½ inch (0·0125 m.)
Hole 1 (lowest). Diam. ¼ inch (0·006 m.). Distance 16⅞ in. (0·431 m.)
Hole 2.   „   „   14⅞ in. (0·379 m.)
Hole 3.   „   „   12⅞ in. (0·328 m.)
(Distance measured from mouth end to upper edge of hole.)

3. IMIN-E, Erudu Tablet: A.J.S.L. xxxix (p. 161), no. 1, col. 11, 33, IV, 26; Chiera, S.R.T. no. 1, ob. col. 11, 24; Demetrius Phalereus (or Dionysius Halicarnassus), 71, *De Elocutione*, quoted by Chappell, *Hist. of Music*, p. 53, note; "Septem discrimina vocum", Virgil, *Aeneid*, VI, 646. Beni-Hasan flutes: Garstang, *Burial Customs*, p. 154; Southgate, *Musical News*, 1903, pp. 102–4 (needing revision). Correct measurements as follows:

Flute A. Length 0·9652 m. (c. 38 inches—Note E). In. diameter 0·015875 m. (c. ⅝ m.).
Hole 1 (lowest).   Diam. 0·005 m.   Distance 0·81 m.
Hole 2.   „   „   0·686 m.
Hole 3.   „   „   0·635 m.
Flute B. Length 0·9144 m. (c. 36 inches—Note F). In. diameter 0·015875 m. (c. ⅝ m.).
Hole 1 (lowest).   Diam. 0·005 m.   Distance 0·76 m.
Hole 2.   „   „   0·633 m.
Hole 3   „   „   0·562 m.

One of these instruments is in the Macgregor Collection, Tamworth; the other is in the Archaeological Institute Coll., Liverpool University.

Hebrew Music: F. L. Cohen, *The Ancient Musical Traditions of the Synagogue* (Trans. of the Musical Association, xix); A. Perlzweig, *Manual of Neginoth* (1912). Indian scale: Fox Strangways, *Music of Hindostan*, p. 104. In Grove's *Dict. of Music* (*s.v.* Indian Music) he states that "at some time before the fourth century B.C. the whole seven notes were taken upwards from C". Shortly afterwards their well-known names are found denoting C, D, E, F♮, G, A (little sharp),

B♮. This scale taken from C (Sa) was called Sa-grāma, but a second scale was taken from F♮ (Ma) and called Ma-grāma: this latter had the sharp fourth (B♮). Since these two scales existed side by side, the old rivalry of the sharp and the perfect fourth was perpetuated, as in China. Corean melodies: Lavignac, *Encyclop. Mus.* Part I, p. 217. S. Arabian scale: Bertram Thomas, *Arabia Felix* (1932), p. 301 and Appendix (the pitch transposed for comparative reference).

4. Ur double-pipes. One of the three pipes is perfect, save for *c.* 3 mm. at the mouth-piece end; they are too fragile to permit straightening out; allowing for this, the measurements are as follows:

Length 0·27 m. (*c.* 10½ inches). In. diameter 0·004 m. (*c.* $\frac{3}{16}$ inch).

Hole 1 (lowest).	Diam. 0·0045 × 0·0035 m.	Distance 0·237 m.
Hole 2.	„ 0·0045 × 0·0035 m.	„ 0·218 m.
Hole 3.	„ 0·0050 × 0·0040 m.	„ 0·188 m.
Hole 4.	„ 0·0060 × 0·0040 m.	„ 0·156 m.

(Distance measured from mouth-piece end to upper edge of hole.)

The reed used for experiment added just under 1½ inches to the length and the lowest note sounded alto c^I (the fundamental of a twelve-inch cylindrical tube closed by a reed). It will be noticed that there is an increase in size in the diameter of the uppermost hole, and the note g^I is decidedly sharp. If this increased size is not due to the straining of the thin silver tubing by fracture, which the normal size of the similar hole on the companion pipe suggests, it is probably intentional; for as one hand only could be used in the double-pipe to support the instrument it was impossible to remove all the fingers, and either the upper hole was half-stopped, a practice not unknown to ancient instrumentalists and which its extended length would facilitate; or else cross-fingering was employed to flatten it to g^I natural, as indicated in the painting of a female pipe-player from Thebes illustrated by Engel, *Music of the Most Ancient Nations*, p. 240.

The pitch of this pipe from Ur is the so-called "continental" (A = 435). The second pipe shows the remains of four holes and was evidently of the same length originally; the mouth-piece end is perfect. The portions of the third pipe are fragmentary. The appearance of three instruments in the grave is not remarkable: in the Leyden examples seven pipes were so found. It is doubtful whether the first harmonics were used, owing to the break of an octave. We are indebted to Dr Legrain of the University Museum, Philadelphia, for the measurements of the Ur pipes.

In dealing with these pipes, as has been said, the scale was obtained by means of a single-beating reed of the Zummarah type; but precisely the same scale resulted with the use of a double-beating reed of straw, similar to remains found in the Egyptian tombs. M. Loret, in Lavignac's *Encyclopédie de la Musique*, Part I, p. 15, maintains that the double-beating reed was used for the single-pipe and the single-beating reed for the double-pipe. His opinion is that the former reed required compression by the lips which is difficult, if not impracticable, with two reeds at the same time. But there is every reason to believe that the reeds were at this early date placed within the cavity of the mouth and beyond the control of the lips. In this case whether it were for a single or for a double-pipe the reed would require a ligature to keep the vibrating edges at their proper distance. Such a ligature was not unknown to the Egyptians, as shown in the illustration given by M. Loret and in later representations of the *aulos*. Even "cut" wire was in frequent use among the Sumerians. These little ligatures were retained in mediaeval times for those instruments on which the reed was placed beneath a cap, and it is still found on the Western European bagpipe-chanter. From the easy and sure way in which the scale was produced on the very slender Ur pipes with a double-beating reed fitted with a ligature, we are led to believe that it was the reed used for such pipes in Mesopotamia as in Egypt. On the other hand the characteristic reed for the covered pipes and bagpipe-chanters of Nearer Asia and Eastern Europe is the single-beating reed, and we conclude that the Babylonian covered pipe (*KITMU*) and probably the crooked pipe (*PITU*) employed a similar reed. The novelty of the *IMBUBU* therefore was not a question of the reed used, but of the shape of the pipe, conical instead of cylindrical.

5. Mongol scale: Van Aalst, *Chinese Music*, p. 15. Russian Finns: Dr M. Guthrie, *Ancient Instruments of Music in remote Russian Villages* (1795) (Brit. Mus. Add. MSS. 14390). Berbers of

Morocco: A. Chottin, *Musique Chleuhs* (Zeitschrift für Vergleichende Musikwissenschaft, I, p. 11).
Highland pipe scale: A. J. Ellis, *Musical Scales of Various Nations* (J.S.A. 1885); ordinary tutors
for the instrument treat the chanter scale of G as normal, but the "fourth" is clearly sharp.

6. Notation: Dr Joh. Wolf, *Handbuch der Notationskunde*, I; Abdy Williams, *Notation*; Gevaert,
Hist. de la Musique de l'Antiquité, I, p. 394; David and Lussy, *Histoire de la Notation Musicale*, p. 2:
"c'est l'alphabet qui a fourni aux premiers peuples les éléments graphiques servant à la représentation des sons". The *Canntaireachd* or syllabic notation used in the ancient bagpipe music of
Scotland took various forms, but it would appear that the known and fixed sounds were originally
represented alphabetically: for instance, the chanter scale G, A, B, C♯, D, E, F♯, G, A, which
corresponds to the Sumerian or Asiatic type, was denoted by the syllabic sounds "em, en, io"
and the vowels "o, a, e, ue, i, I". Although various consonants were added before and after
each of them to express "grace-notes", the fundamental sound remained the same. It may have
been derived from a yet earlier harp notation; for, if the lowest string (C) of the harp were
denoted by the letter A and the letters I and J were treated as identical (which they are), on
a diatonically tuned instrument M, N and O would fall on the "em" (G), "en" (A) and "io"
(B) of the bagpipe scale. For fuller information cf. J. F. Campbell, *Canntaireachd* or Articulate
Music; J. P. Grant, *Canntaireachd* (Music and Letters, VI, 1925), and the publications of the
Piobaireachd Society of Glasgow. W. L. Manson, *The Highland Bagpipe*, devotes a chapter to
this somewhat intricate subject.

7. Notation tablet, KAR. I, 4: Dr Ebeling, *Religiöse Texte aus Assur*, I, 4; Bezold, P.S.B.A.
x, 8, pp. 423ff.; *Zeitschrift der Deutschen Morgenländischen Gesellschaft*, LXX, pp. 532ff.; Langdon,
Le Poème Sumérien du Paradis, pp. 42ff.; A. Jeremias, *Das alte Testament* (1930), pp. 20ff.; C. Sachs,
Sitzungsberichte der Preussischen Akademie der Wissenschaften, *Die Entzifferung einer Bab. Noten-
schrift*, XVIII (1924); also *Musik des Altertums*, pp. 40ff.; B. Landsberger, Festschrift Max von
Oppenheim, *Archiv für Orientforschung*, I (1933), *Die angebliche Bab. Notenschrift*; Hen. de Genouillac,
R.A. XXV, p. 124, *Curieux Syllabaire de la Dynastie de Babylone* (an Akkadian-Sumerian Lexicon);
R. E. van der Meer, *Textes scolaires de Suse*, Mém. de la Miss. Archéol. de Suse, Paris (1935).

8. Sumerian pictographs: C. J. Gadd, *Sumerian Reading Book*, Introd. p. 10. The following
example taken from the opening eight lines of the hymn and its notation will explain the de-
ciphering process adopted throughout. The literal translation of the Sumerian text is adopted
from C. J. Gadd's *Sumerian Reading Book*, p. 133: the signs are those given in the older Sippar
text, as transcribed by Scheil, *Une Saison de fouilles à Sippar*, pp. 38–40.

1. "When in heaven and earth the steadfast twain had been completed."
   Notation signs ME and PA, meaning "Mother" (earth) and "Father" (sky or heaven).
2. "And the goddess-mother Inanna she (too) had been created."
   Notation sign A (repeated five times), meaning "Begetter."
3. "When the earth had been laid down in the place made (for it)."
   Notation signs KU and DIB, meaning "to place" and "to fasten" as a stone in its setting
   [DIB might be read also as LU, but "to be puffed up" belies the context].
4. "When the designs of heaven and earth had been decided."
   Notation sign MAŠ, meaning "the pair" (i.e. heaven and earth).
5. "And, watercourse and canal straight to set."
   Notation signs MAŠ and ZAL, meaning "the two glittering ones."
6. "The rivers Tigris and Euphrates, their banks had been appointed."
   Notation signs SI, ZAL, and A, meaning "to enclose, glittering, water".
7. "(When) Anu, Enlil, Utu and Enki."
   Notation signs U and BAR (not MAŠ as above) meaning "Masters" "behold".
8. "The great gods."
   Notation signs LAL, IGI BAR, meaning "look, with the eye (of favour), behold".

This suppliant attitude, during the mention of the great gods or their relations to mortals, is
characteristic and occurs again in other lines where the bounteous Lady of Heaven or the All-
commanding Father are mentioned.

9. Acrophony: Isaac Taylor, *The Alphabet*, I, p. 43; M. Sprengling, *The Alphabet*, Oriental Institute Communications, no. 12, Chicago University Press, 1931. Professor Landsberger in the *Oppenheim Festschrift* (1933) considers these detached syllables as a secret priestly code. When isolated from their context, such signs could easily have been thus adapted; indeed, Genouillac's "curieux syllabaire" (p. 95) and other tablets suggest it. Ras Shamra: H. Bauer, *Das Alphabet von Ras Shamra* (1932), *Syria* (Paris), XIV, p. 230. Tell Duweir inscriptions (Lachish): J. L. Starkey, *Illustrated London News*, Aug. 10, 1935. The alphabetical cuneiform of Ras Shamra is interesting as showing another early attempt to use these syllabic signs for an alphabetical language. Although some of them may be read acrophonically, their selection does not appear to have been made on these lines, but solely for their simplicity and clearness in writing. To the uninstructed Babylonian or Assyrian the meaning of the words thus formed must have been unintelligible. In our own age efforts have been made to show the derivation of our present alphabet from the ancient cuneiform: cf. Hommel, *Geschichte Babyloniens*, and P.S.B.A. (1893).

10. Before deciding to adopt the direct alphabetical interpretation of the signs, we endeavoured to unravel them on the lines of the earliest Greek system (Gevaert, *Hist. Mus.* I, p. 394), which was certainly neither the simplest nor most obvious form, but connected with the peculiar tuning of the Greek lyre: it produced, however, only chaotic results as applied to the cuneiform signs, and the placing of A (aleph) on the *highest* note of the scale seemed fatal to it. In the eleventh century of our era Adebold proposed the use of the whole alphabet consecutively as a system of notation, placing A on the lowest note. Thus history repeats itself. Cf. Grove, *Dict. Mus. s.v. Notation*. For unison and octave singing, cf. Aristotle, *Problemata*, Sect. XIX, 17, 18, 39, 40; Plato, *De Legibus*, VII, 16. The question of the use of harmony has been raised by Dr Curt Sachs in *Eine Ägyptische Winkelharfe* (Zeitschrift für Ägyptische Sprache und Altertumskunde, LXIX, pp. 68 ff.). In his paper on the Sumerian "Notation" Signs he concluded that the harpist constantly used octaves, double octaves, fifths, fourths and even seconds, in the accompaniment of the hymn. In his later paper (1933), wherein he takes as his subject a specimen of the Assyrian triangular harp found in Egypt and now in the Museum of Musical Instruments at the Hochschule für Musik, Berlin (Pl. VI, 1, 2), he again affirms, from the position of the hands of the seventh century players shown in the so-called Elamite Orchestra of the time of Assurbanipal (Pl. VI, 8), that fifths and fourths were sounded as chords: but the position of the hand *alone* cannot be taken as sufficient proof, since the fingers of the player are naturally extended for plucking the strings of the harp and obtaining the necessary "grip". Van Aalst (*Chinese Music*, p. 24), however, says that fourths, fifths and octaves were played on the *Kin* and *Sê*: though the music was written in the simplest manner, the players on these psalteries were allowed to "embellish their part with all the difficulties which their skill would allow". In the score of the hymn in honour of Confucius the *Kin* plays in fourths and fifths and the *Sê* in octaves and fifths. When single notes are struck, they are repeated in quick succession to sustain the sound, as in our interpretation of the Babylonian notation. It is interesting also to notice that in another official score, the flutes and pipes hold sustained fourths and fifths, which may suggest a similar practice on the double-pipes of antiquity with their limited scale and small compass of a "fourth" or a "fifth". See Bishop G. E. Moule, J.R.A.S. (North China Branch), XXXIII, *Notes on the half-yearly Sacrifice to Confucius*.

CHAPTER V

THE APPRECIATION OF MUSIC

As references to the tablets which mention the use of each musical instrument have already been given under their respective headings in Chapters I–III, they are not repeated here. The present chapter deals more particularly with the musical aspect of the Sumerian and Akkadian ritual; further details with respect to the temple buildings and general organization will be found in such works as these: L. W. King, *History of Sumer and Akkad*, pp. 265 ff.; S. Langdon, *Babylonian Liturgies* (1913) and *Sumerian Liturgies and Psalms* (1919); L. Legrain, *The Culture of the*

Babylonians (Pennsylvania Museum, Bab. Sect. Publications, xiv, 1925); Curt Sachs, *Musik des Altertums* (1924), p. 39; M. Jastrow, *Bildermappe zur Religion Babyloniens* (1912); also *Religion of Babylonia and Assyria*; L. Spence, *Myths and Legends of Babylonia and Assyria*. For a form of serpent-worship cf. Frankfort, *Religion in Babylonia* (Tell Asmar Report), *Illustrated London News*, Sept. 5, 1936. For the oldest representation of a temple cf. *Ur Excavations*, iii, p. 35, no. 389.

1. Hymn of Lamentation: Langdon, B.L. xix, ll. 28–33. Wisdom of Ea: Langdon, S.B.P. p. 176, 27. Use of lyre at funerals: *Gudea Statue* B, v, 1, "ki-mah-uru-ka al-nu-gar".

2. Double-pipe, timbrel and drums in worship: Macmillan, B.A. v, p. 581, and Langdon, S.B.P. 68, 5; 70, 15. Devil-driving: C. L. Woolley, J.R.A.S. (1926), p. 707.

3. Bartholomaeus: Hawkins, *Hist. Music*, book vii, ch. 60; C. J. Gadd, *Monuments of Ur* (1929), p. 36. Witches: M. Murray, *The God of the Witches* (1933). "Oozer": Udal, *Dorsetshire Folklore*, p. 97. Hierakonpolis plaque: Lavignac, *Dict. Music*, Part i, p. 14. Mummers: J. Bonomi, *Nineveh*, p. 230. Turin Papyrus: Chappell, *Hist. Music*, p. 399; Boethius, *De Consolatione Philosophiae*, book i, Prose 4. *Troilus and Creseide*, i, 730 ff. *Rāvanahasta*: C. Sachs, *Die Musikinstrumente Indiens*, p. 112, fig. 76. Plutarch (Reiske Ed.), vii, p. 481.

4. Chinese drums in worship: Bishop G. E. Moule, J.R.A.S. (North China Branch), xxxiii, p. 18; Stanford and Forsyth, *History of Music*, p. 35. Foundation Ritual: Weissbach, *Miscell.* 32 and pl. 12; Langdon, B.L. (1913), Introd. ix.

5. Sumerian and Assyrian songs: Langdon, J.R.A.S. (1921), p. 12; E. Ebeling, *Ein Hymnen-Katalog aus Assur* (1923), also *Religiöse Keilschrift-texte aus Assur*, xxviii, no. 158.

CHAPTER VI

THE RACIAL ELEMENT IN MUSIC

1. Ethnology and Music: E. v. Hornbostel, Zeitschrift für Ethnologie (1911 and 1914), *The Ethnology of African Sound Instruments* (Africa, vol. vi, no. 3); C. Sachs, *Geist und Werden der Musik-instrumente*; R. Lachmann, *Musik des Orients*; J. Kunst, *Papuan Music*; P. R. Kirby, *The Musical Instruments of the Native Races of S. Africa*; E. Mackay, *Indus Civilization* (1935).

2. Sumerian origins. Abyssinia or North-east Africa: W. J. Perry, *The Growth of Civilization*, and *Man*, xxix, 18; Turkestan: Ungnad, *Wiener Zeitschrift für die Kunde des Morgenlandes*, xxxiv (1927); Persia or Baluchistan: Frankfort, *Archaeology and the Sumerian Problem* (Studies in Ancient Oriental Civilization, Chicago University, no. 4, 1932); Pliny, N.H. ii, 109; Berosus: Cory's *Ancient Fragments* (1832). Dravidians: Hall, *Near East*, p. 174. Proto-Arabs: Sir A. Keith, *Ur Excavation Report*, ii, pp. 400 ff. (1934). Indus Valley: Gordon Childe, *New Light on the Most Ancient East* (1934). Earliest inhabitants of S. Mesopotamia: Semites or Hurrians: Speiser, *Mesopotamian Origins*, p. 81. Arab type: Keith, *Al Ubaid*, p. 216. Elamites: Campbell Thompson, *Archaeologia*, lxx, pp. 110 ff. Sumerians: Frankfort, *Archaeology and the Sumerian Problem* (1932). Subaraic Culture: Oppenheim, *Tell Halaf*, p. 48 (1933). "Land of the Reeds": Prince, *Materials for a Sumerian Lexicon*, p. 206. Language affinities. Turkish: Hommel, *Innsbrucker Jahrbuch für Völkerkunde*, i (1926). Bantu: *Festschrift für Pater Schmidt*, Vienna, 1928. Caucasian: Tseretheli, *Sumerian and Georgian*, J.R.A.S. 1913 (pp. 783 ff.); 1914, p. 1; 1915, p. 250; 1916, p. 1. Chinese: C. J. Ball, *Chinese and Sumerian* (1913). Dravidian and Mediterranean peoples—an ancient connection: A. C. Haddon, *The Races of Man*, p. 109. Dravidians show a mixture with Eurasiatics (Alpines), Haddon, *l.c.* p. 111.•Indus Valley Civilization: Marshall, Mackay and others; Gordon Childe, *New Light on the Most Ancient East*, ch. viii (1934). Keith: "One can still trace the ancient Sumerian face eastwards among the inhabitants of Afghanistan and Baluchistan, until the Valley of the Indus is reached some 1500 miles distant from Mesopotamia." *Al-Ubaid*, p. 216.

3. Illustrations of archaic Egyptian reed-pipes: Quibell, *Hierakonpolis*, ii, pl. 28. Sistrum: Balfour, *Instruments of the Malay Peninsula* (1908), pl. xx, fig. 1. Blowing horns: Hornbostel, *Ethnology of African Instruments*, "Africa", vi, p. 292.

4. Further details in *Music and Letters*, x, pp. 108 ff. by Galpin, *The Sumerian Harp of Ur* (1929). Indian bow-shaped harp: G. R. Hunter, *Script of Harappa* (p. 206); Marshall, *Mohenjo-daro*, Pl. cv. Sumerians in Arabia: *Music and Letters, l.c.* p. 118, note 27. Hatshepsut's fleet: *Music and Letters, l.c.* p. 119, no. 28. Baganda funeral rites: J. Roscoe, *The Baganda* (1911), pp. 107 ff. Egyptian *ZAKKAL* or upright harp: Lavignac, *Encyl. Mus.* Part I, figs. 59, 60. [Dr Contenau, Conservateur of the Egyptian Antiquities, has carefully examined this specimen in the Louvre and states that there is provision made in the sound-board for only twenty-one strings.] Stainer, *Music of the Bible*, pl. v. The Persian form of the sixth century A.D. is well illustrated by R. K. Porter, *Travels in Georgia, Persia, etc.* (1824). Buddhist form: Yetts, *Cat. Eumorfopoulos Coll.* III. Chinese harp: *New China Review*, Hong Kong, 1912: F. T. Piggott, *The Musical Instruments of Japan*, p. 151. Cambodian harp: Mahillon, *Cat. of the Instrumental Collection*, Conserv. Music, Brussels, II, 15. Moorish harp: J. F. Riaño, *Notes on Early Spanish Music*, 1887. Turkish harp: Engel, *Cat. S. Kensington Museum* (1872), p. 58. Ostyak harp: C. Sach's, *Real Lexicon, s.v.* Shotang: also *Handbuch der Musikinstrumentenkunde* (1920), p. 231. For the development of the Clarseth or North European harp see Galpin, *Old English Instruments of Music* (3rd ed. 1932), ch. I.

A SUMERIAN HYMN ON THE CREATION OF MAN
With harp accompaniment of the second millennium B.C.

(The singer, no doubt, ornamented his part with grace-notes as in the ancient Indian chanting, and the intervals, taken in ascent by a skip, were rendered in descent with a light slide. The crotchet notation has no definite time-value; it merely denotes melodic progressions. Rhythm and stress depend on the words. The small numbers mark the hymn lines. For Sumerian pronunciation see p. xi.)

(61) gašam gašam ug-ni ug-ni (62) še-dim ni-bi-ne ki-ta si-sig-ki dim

men, wise in letters, brave in deeds, shall rise, *like ears of corn self-springing from the ground;*

(61) (62)

pa ga pa pa ga a a ur an an

(63) nig-nu-kur-ru mul da-er-šu (64) ud-gig-na-ta ezen Dingir-e-ne šu-du-a

while, fix'd in their eternal seats, the stars *revolve the round of holy feast and fast.*

(63) (64)

ni ni ni ni a

(65) ni-te-a-ni giš-ḫar ga-gal-la (66) mûn-ḫa-ḫar-ri (67) An Dingir En-lil

This, of their own unfetter'd will, the Gods *have so decreed;* *by An and by En-lil*

(65) (66) (67)

ni ni ni ni ni ni a ab ba ab ba mu

(68) Dingir En-ki Dingir Nin-maḫ (69) Dingir ga-gal-e-ne (70) ki nam-lu-galu ba-rìn-dim-eš

By Enki and Ninmakh, Almighty Gods. *Here too, where men first drew their living breath,*

(68) (69) (70)

ab ba zal ab ba a ab ba gir ku ku ku ku ku

(71) Dingir Nisaba ki-bi nam-en-nâm-gub

All bounteous Nisaba hath set her sway.

(71)

ku ku ku ku a

INDEX AND GLOSSARY

PLATE I

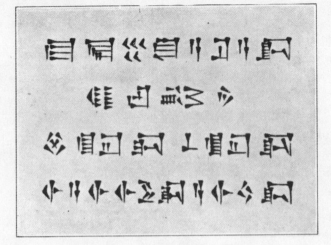

"Musick's Ministerie"
A Sumerian appreciation in cuneiform script; *c.* 2400 B.C. (see p. vii)

A Sumerian Banquet with music and song
From the Royal Standard, Ur; *c.* 2700 B.C.   British Museum

PLATE II. MUSICAL SUBJECTS ON EARLY SEALS

1. **Lyre and Dancing Sticks**
   From a Royal Tomb, Ur; *c.* 2700 B.C.   Baghdad Museum

2. **Monkey with Reed-pipe**
   From a Royal Tomb, Ur; *c.* 2700 B.C.   Baghdad Museum

3. **Lyre, Sistrum, Timbrel and Drum-shaped Altar**
   Agade Period; *c.* 2500 B.C.   The Louvre, Paris

4. **Bow-shaped Harp and Timbrel**
   Queen Shubad's Tomb, Ur; *c.* 2700 B.C.   University Museum, Philadelphia

5. **Lyre, Flute, Rattle and Drum**
   From the Royal Cemetry, Ur; *c.* 2700 B.C.   University Museum, Philadelphia

PLATE II

1

2

3

4

5

PLATE III. DRUMS, TIMBRELS AND BELLS

1. **Large Drum and Horn**
   Carchemish Relief; *c.* 1250 B.C.   British Museum (portion)

2. **Kettle-Drum and Cymbals**
   Babylonian Plaque; *c.* 1100 B.C.   British Museum

3. **Large Timbrel**
   Nippur Figurine; *c.* 2000 B.C.   University Museum, Philadelphia

4. **Tablet showing Kettle-Drum**
   From Erech; *c.* 300 B.C.   Brussels Museum

5. **Small Timbrel**
   Babylonian Figurine; *c.* 2000 B.C.   British Museum

6. **Large Drum**
   Stele of Ur-Nammu; *c.* 2270 B.C.   University Museum, Philadelphia

7. **Hour-glass-shaped Drum**
   Babylonian Figurine; *c.* 2000 B.C.   British Museum

8. **Horse Bell**
   From Nineveh; *c.* 700 B.C.   British Museum

9. **Incantation Bell**
   From Babylonia; *c.* 600 B.C.   Berlin Museum

PLATE III

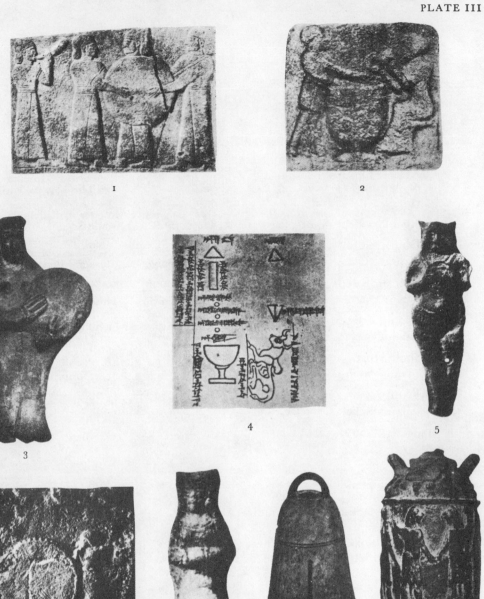

1

2

3

4

5

6

7

8

9

PLATE IV. FLUTES, PIPES AND HORNS

1. Vertical Flute
   Archaic Sumerian Seal   The Louvre, Paris

2. Whistle
   From Birs Nimrûd, Babylon   Formerly Royal Asiatic Society, London

3. Double Reed-pipes
   From the Older Cemetery, Ur; *c.* 2800 B.C.   University Museum, Philadelphia

4. Double Reed-pipes
   Nippur Figurine; *c.* 2000 B.C.   University Museum, Philadelphia

5. Crooked Reed-pipes
   Susian Figurine; *c.* 750 B.C.   The Louvre, Paris

6. Shell Horn
   From Nineveh; *c.* 700 B.C.   British Museum

7. Trumpet
   Assyrian Relief; *c.* 700 B.C.   British Museum

PLATE IV

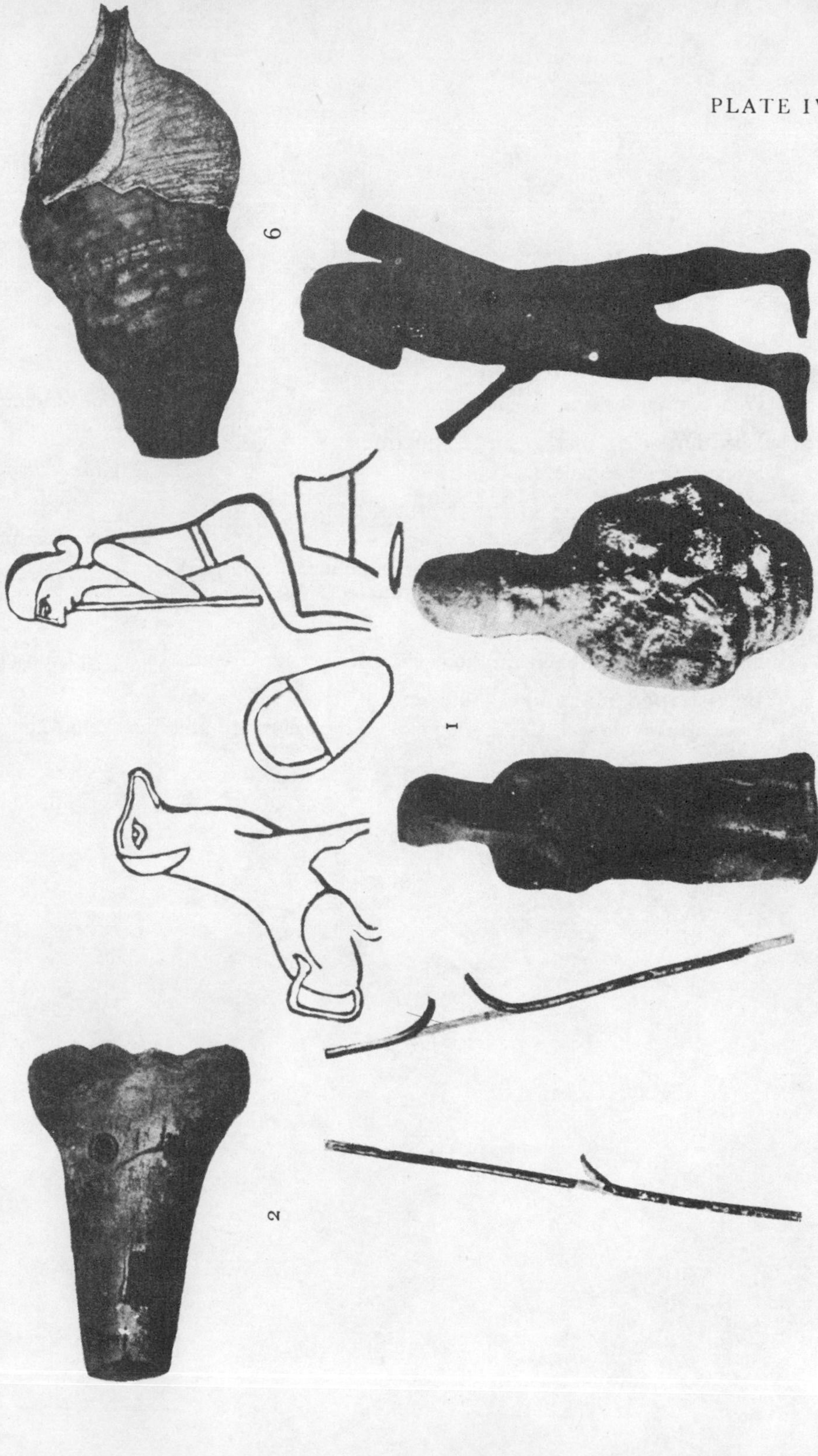

PLATE·V. BOW-SHAPED HARPS

1. **Small Bow-shaped Harp**
    From a vase, Bismya; *c.* 3200 B.C.   Istambul Museum

2. **Line Drawing of the same specimen**
    From Bismya; *c.* 3200 B.C.   E. J. Banks, *Bismya*

3. **Large Bow-shaped Harp (restored)**
    From the Royal Cemetery, Ur; *c.* 2700 B.C.   British Museum
    A, B. Border and terminal plaque of soundboard (enlarged).
    C, D. Section and contour of body (restored).

4. **Bow-shaped Harp**
    From stone slab, Khafage; *c.* 3000 B.C.   University Oriental Institute, Chicago

5. **Bow-shaped Harp and Clappers**
    From an archaic seal, Ur; *c.* 2800 B.C.   University Museum, Philadelphia

PLATE V

1

2

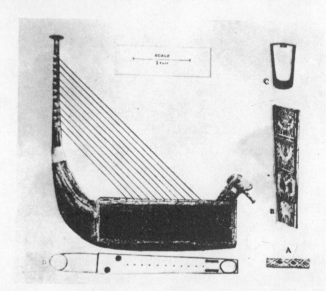

3

4

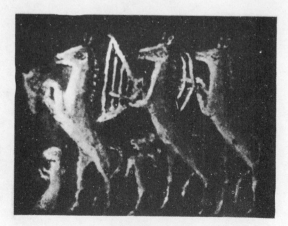

5

PLATE VI.
HORIZONTAL HARPS, UPRIGHT HARPS AND LYRES

1. **Upright Harp**
   From an Egyptian Tomb; *c.* 700 B.C.   Musikinstr. Museum, Berlin

2. **Upright Harp**
   Reconstruction of the above specimen   Musikinstr. Museum, Berlin

3. **Upright Harp and Square Timbrel**
   From bronze vessel, Niḥawand, Persia; *c.* 2200 B.C.   Prof. E. Herzfeld

4. **Horizontal Harp**
   Nippur Plaque; *c.* 2000 B.C.   University Museum, Philadelphia

5. **Horizontal Harp**
   From an Egyptian Tomb; *c.* 1000 B.C.   Florence Museum

6. **Upright Harp**
   Sippar Figurine; *c.* 1900 B.C.   Istambul Museum

7. **Lyres, Timbrel and Cymbals**
   From an Assyrian Bas-relief; *c.* 680 B.C.   The Louvre, Paris

8. **Upright Harp, Horizontal Harp and Double-pipe**
   Assyrian Bas-relief; *c.* 680 B.C.   British Museum

PLATE VI

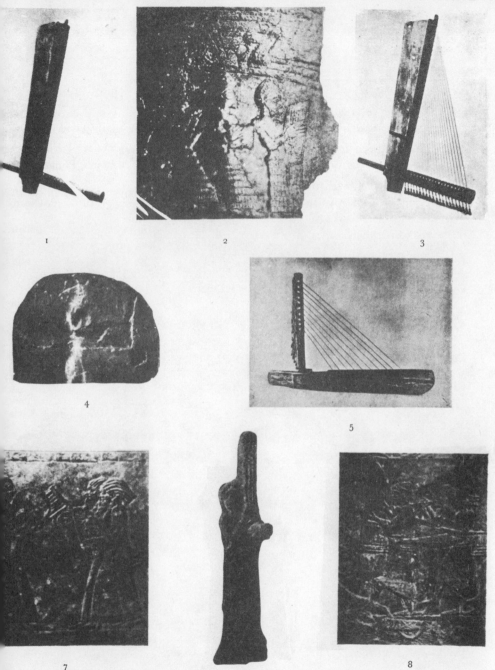

1

2

3

4

5

7

6

8

PLATE VII. LYRES FROM UR

1. Gold Lyre (restored)
   From the Royal Cemetery; *c.* 2700 B.C.   Baghdad Museum

2. Boat-shaped Lyre
   From the Royal Cemetery; *c.* 2700 B.C.   University Museum, Philadelphia

3. Silver Lyre, with original tuning rods
   From the Royal Cemetery; *c.* 2700 B.C.   British Museum

PLATE VII

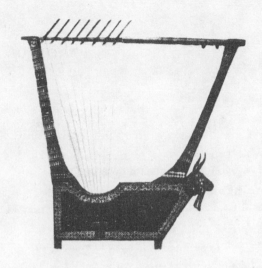

I

2

3

PLATE VIII. LYRES, LUTES AND PSALTERIES

1. **Lyre (simple type)**
   Tell Halaf, N. Syria (third millennium B.C.)   Berlin Museum

2. **Lyre, Sistrum and Square Timbrel**
   Plaque, Royal Cemetery, Ur; *c.* 2700 B.C.   University Museum, Philadelphia

3. **Lyre**
   From a bas-relief, Lagash (Tello); *c.* 2400 B.C.   The Louvre, Paris

4. **"Bagana" Lyre with tuning rods**
   Abyssinia; nineteenth cent. A.D.   S. Kensington Museum

5. **Psalteries, Timbrel and Double-pipe**
   Ivory box, Nimrûd; *c.* 800 B.C.   British Museum

6. **Long-necked Lute**
   Nippur Plaque; *c.* 1900 B.C.   University Museum, Philadelphia

7. **Long-necked Lute**
   Babylonian Boundary Stone, Susa; *c.* 1600 B.C.   The Louvre, Paris

PLATE VIII

1

2

3

4

5

6

7

1. Obverse.

2. Reverse.

PLATE IX

PLATE IX. ASSHUR TABLET WITH NOTATION

C. 800 B.C.   Staatliches Museum, Berlin

1. Obverse.
2. Reverse.